J. Hucks

A Pedestrian Tour Through North Wales

In a Series of Letters

J. Hucks

A Pedestrian Tour Through North Wales
In a Series of Letters

ISBN/EAN: 9783744759502

Printed in Europe, USA, Canada, Australia, Japan

Cover: Foto ©Thomas Meinert / pixelio.de

More available books at **www.hansebooks.com**

A
PEDESTRIAN TOUR

THROUGH

NORTH WALES,

IN A

SERIES OF LETTERS.

By J. HUCKS, B. A.

With gold and gems if Chilian mountains glow,
If bleak and barren Cambria's hills arife,
There plague and poifon, luft and rapine grow,
Here peaceful are the vales, and pure the fkies,
And freedom fire the foul, and fparkles in the eyes.

THE MINSTREL.

London:

Printed for J. DEBRETT, Piccadilly; and J.
EDWARDS, Pall Mall.

Sold alfo by W. H. LUNN, B. FLOWER, and J. DEIGHTON,
Cambridge; Meffrs. BINNS, and GREENWOOD, Leeds;
and Meffrs. DYER, and TREWMAN, Exeter.

1795.

PREFACE.

A T a time fo peculiarly alarming to the affairs of this country, that every hour comes attended with fome frefh calamity: when reafon and juftice are fuffering in the conflict of nations: when rapine and oppreffion are defolating the faireft regions of Europe: in fhort, when the common interefts of humanity, when every dear and invaluable privilege, that can render fociety lovely and defirable, is

altogether

altogether neglected or forgotten, and the happy re-union of liberty and tranquillity, more the object of our wishes than our expectations; in such an eventful, but fatal, period of the political drama, the following letters may probably be confidered as an intrufion upon the public attention, too much abforbed in the nice intrigues of the cabinet and the field, to unbend their thoughts to lighter purfuits, when the great fcale of our political exiftence is in danger of finking for ever.

Left any fuch argument fhould be adduced againft him, the author begs leave

leave to make one obfervation, (viz.)
That he has written neither for the
ftatefman, the general, or the politi-
cian; he is fenfible, that from the
nature of the fubject, his little work
will not be extended amongft a very
large clafs of readers; the amufement
of an individual was originally the
fole object of the following letters,
but he has ventured to make them
public, under the hope that they may,
in fome meafure, contribute to the
fatisfaction of thofe who have not feen,
yet may wifh to become familiar with,
the outlines of a country, fo diffimilar
in every refpect to England; and to
whom a flight fketch of the moft

prominent

prominent features of its inhabitants,
may not appear either tedious or un-
interesting; and he flatters himself,
they will not be unacceptable to those,
who, like himself, might be induced to
explore the beautiful scenery of North
Wales; and to whom the short,
though probably imperfect account
of it there given, may prove an useful
companion, to direct them in their
progress through a country, to which
they might be altogether unacquainted.

He claims the indulgence of his
readers for the tautology and egotism,
almost inseparable from works of such
a descrip-

a defcription; but he has, as much as
poffible, endeavoured to avoid a repetition of names, and for this reafon,
has, in moft cafes, fpoken of himfelf as being the only fpectator; at
the fame time, in juftice to thofe who
accompanied him, he takes this opportunity of acknowledging himfelf,
upon many occafions, greatly indebted
to them for many interefting remarks
and ufeful information, which otherwife he could not have had the means
of acquiring.

Since he firft conceived the defign
of publifhing thefe letters, fome neceffary additions have been made, and
a fhort

a fhort Appendix added, for the fake
of giving them a more connected
form; for there were a few places,
which, owing to particular circumftances, it was not in his power to
fee, and a fhort account of thefe, together with fome other detached obfervations, compofe the Appendix, to
which alfo are fubjoined the names of
the moft noted places that they vifited
in the courfe of their route, and their
diftances from each other. Thofe
marked with one or more afterifks,
imply the number of nights they remained at each.

A
PEDESTRIAN TOUR,

&c. &c. &c.

LETTER I.

BALA, North Wales, July 11, 1794.

SURROUNDED on all fides by cloud-capt mountains; arrived amongft a people, to whofe language I am a perfect ftranger, and whofe manners and cuftoms are as eccentric as they are fingular, every circumftance attracts attention, and every object excites admiration. But it is with pleafure, my dear friend, that I ceafe for a while from contemplating the fcene around me, and turn to that

B   which

which I have so lately quitted: memory willingly lingers round a spot where the mind has not been much oppressed with sorrow or care; and I must, in justice, acknowledge, that during a residence of three years at Cambridge, the happiness I there enjoyed was scarcely ever interrupted, or overshadowed even by the smallest cloud of misfortune; a retrospect will therefore prove to me a constant source of satisfaction, because the memory of the past will not be accompanied with images of regret, or any other cause of sorrow or reproach. It will be peculiarly pleasing to me to write to you from time to time, and give you some account of our "Travels' History," to relate to you all our "most disastrous chances and moving accidents by flood or field;" for in every thing which concerned us, you were pleased to express yourself particularly interested,

and

and I affure you, it is not alone in compli-
ance with your earneft and repeated requeft, but under the immediate impulfe
of my own wifhes and inclination, that I
am now induced to write to you.

The mode of travelling which we have
adopted, at the firft view promifes nothing remarkably alluring; and I think
you were of opinion that our refolution
was not equal to the undertaking of fuch
an enterprife, and treated the whole plan
as vifionary and romantic. But I flatter
myfelf you will now be convinced we are
in earneft, efpecially when I tell you that
experience has more than ever confirmed
us in our original intention; for the pleafure we have hitherto derived from our
progrefs, has much exceeded our moft
fanguine expectations.

I fhall

I shall now proceed to give you a short detail of occurrences, from the day on which my compagnon de voyage and myself departed from Cambridge, to the present time. Behold us, then, more like two pilgrims performing a journey to the tomb of some wonder-working saint, than men travelling for their pleasure and amusement. We are so completely metamorphosed, that I much doubt whether you would recognise us through our disguise; we carry our clothes, &c. in a wallet or knapsack, from which we have not hitherto experienced the slightest inconvenience: as for all ideas of appearance and gentility, they are entirely out of the question—our object is to see, not to be seen; and if I thought I had one acquaintance who would be ashamed of me and my knapsack, seated by the fire side of an honest Welsh peasant, in a country

village,

village, I fhould not only make myfelf perfectly eafy on my own account, but fhould be induced to pity and defpife him for his weaknefs.

We made fome ftay at Oxford, where we experienced the utmoft hofpitality and attention; and then profecuted our route by way of Glocefter, Rofs, Hereford, Bifhop's Caftle, &c. I have annexed the names of the places we have paffed through in their regular order, as well as their diftances from each other, fo that you will perceive we have not fatigued ourfelves with very long marches.

It is not my intention to trouble you with a minute defcription of places; or with uninterefting accounts of individuals, from which you would not derive any very defirable information in the perufal,

nor

nor I any gratification in the relation.
The feelings of men generally harmonize
with their fituation; and fublime images
muft naturally arife in the mind, when the
external objects of its contemplation are
accompanied with any thing peculiarly
grand or majeftic: under fuch impreffions
I cannot, when I am upon the fummit of
a mountain, with a beautiful and fertile
country widely extending upon the fight,
think of any thing but the profpect before me; nor in admiring a cathedral
conftructed with all the elegance of fi-
nifhed architecture, could I reduce my
thoughts to the rule and compafs in order
to meafure its height and dimenfions, or
enter into a critique upon the juftnefs of
its proportions; the form would triumph
over the matter, and drive every other
confideration to a diftance: and after
contemplating the venerable remains of

fome

fome once celebrated fabric, I could not patiently endure to give an hiſtorical detail of its founder, the different benefactors to whom it has been indebted, or the charters and privileges it has enjoyed. But they are not alone ſublime ſituations which excite ſublime ideas; every object in nature is intereſting, and wherever nature is, I feel ſimilar ſenſations; mountains and valleys, rivers and rivulets, nay the ſmalleſt plants that are trodden under our feet, unſeen or unregarded, are inexhauſtible ſources, to a contemplative mind, of gratification and delight.

O how can'ſt thou renounce the boundleſs ſtore
Of charms, which nature to her vot'ry yields !
The warbling woodland, the refounding ſhore,
The pomp of groves, and garniture of fields ;
All that the genial ray of morning gilds,
And all that echoes to the ſong of even ;
All that the mountain's ſheltering boſom ſhields,
And all the dread magnificence of heaven ;
O how can'ſt thou renounce, and hope to be forgiven !
The Minſtrel.

Let

Let the atheift or the *manicheift* (if fuch
there are in reality, as I know there are
fome profeffedly), pay a little attention to
the philofophy of nature, ever changing,
but ftill connected, at once majeftic but
fimple, difdaining the rules and frigid
boundaries of art, at the fame time mo-
delled upon the moft beautiful and grace-
ful proportion—their fhort-lived doubts
muft inftantly vanifh, and their daring incredulity yield to the moft rational and
forcible conviction ; they muft then confefs that this world could never have been
created by chance, or be the work of a
malignant deity; but that it bears the
traces of a hand divine, the beautiful pro-
duction of a benevolent, eternal, and intellectual being. I can fcarcely believe
there is that man exifting, who can
fee without emotion the beauteous orb of
day rifing in the eaft, and in the evening
behold

behold its fetting beams; who can look with apathy upon the moon when fhe gilds the brow of night, and all the numerous hoft of ftars, the panoply of heaven, that fhine around her; who equally unmoved by ftorms and funfhine, by calms and tempefts, can yet be induced, from a pitiful and weak defpair of a happy futurity, from a wilful incredulity, or a mifguided fcepticifm, to deny the great and generating caufe of all effects! The chief object of this expedition, and from which I hope to derive the greateft pleafure, is to explore the hidden beauties of nature unmechanized by the ingenuity of man; as well as to make fome obfervations upon the human character under every different attitude it may affume; in fhort, to ftudy nature in her works, and man in fociety. The lower orders of people in this part of Great Britain have as

yet

yet prefented to me only a picture of humiliation and wretchednefs. Whether this be the general character, or but a partial appearance of the country, I fhall have other opportunities of difcovering in the profecution of my journey: at prefent I am far from entertaining a favourable opinion of their ftock of happinefs; undeniably there are numerous examples of apparent cheerfulnefs and content to be found amongft the poor inhabitants of a mud-built cottage; but are not the focial endearments of domeftic life (the only fource of enjoyment amongft the lower orders of mankind), too often imbittered by repeated difficulties and diftreffes, and rendered fo many aggravating circumftances to the wounded recollection of a parent, furrounded by a numerous and helplefs family who look up to him for protection and fupport, which

he

he is utterly unable to afford them? I believe and hope that such inftances of want and degradation are rare; but very few of them are requifite to convince any man, capable of feeling for others as he would for himfelf, that the aggregate of happinefs, amongft the lower fpecies of our fellow-creatures, does not bear a juft proportion to that of pain, and that their condition is capable of very effential improvement. Under the preffure of poverty and misfortune, the mind oftentimes forgets its noble nature, and the proper degree of eftimation with which it fhould regard its own exiftence: and this is the cafe with that defcription of men here fpoken of. To remove then this evil, by doing away the caufe of the complaint (viz. Oppreffion), would be a work well worthy the attention of every friend of mankind. Under whatever circumftances of poverty

and

and inferiority many of our fellow-creatures may be placed, yet they have a juft
claim upon our protection and fupport ;
for though habit, and the hard hand of
oppreffive want, may have contracted the
modes of thinking amongft them, yet
they undoubtedly poffefs intellects, which,
if properly cultivated, might equally
adorn a fenate, or a forum, with thofe who
are called their fuperiors, from the mere
accidental circumftances of wealth, or
hereditary diftinctions. A human being, as
he comes originally from the hand of nature, is every where the fame ; the capa-
city of improvement, the talents and
virtues which the mind is capable of acquiring and exercifing, are to every ftate
of fociety alike inherent. Surely then all
muft rejoice in the melioration of that
ftate, fince to contribute to its improvement is the nobleft purfuit of individuals,

and

and ought to be the fole end of all governments; but the facred principles of the focial compact are no longer regarded, and
that which fhould be the firft is now become
the laft care or confideration of legiflative
fcience.   To fay that the ftate of fociety
cannot be improved, is either to affert its
perfection, to confefs that all exertions to
improve that ftate would be vain, or that
thefe political evils are either neceffary or
irremediable.   To the firft of thefe argu-
ments, if they can be deemed worthy of
fuch a denomination, there is no neceffity
to reply, becaufe it carries with it its own
conviction; and with refpect to the laft,
no one will hefitate to pronounce it an
impious reflection upon the benevolence
of the Creator, whofe intention could
never be to fubject man to any fpecies of
political tyranny whatever; and well indeed might this fair creation and celeftial
C   harmony

harmony be called a Manichean fyftem, or work of a malevolent being, if he could fanction upon this globe the deteftable crimes, and abhorred impieties committed under the patronage, and often the immediate confequence, of vicious and corrupted governments; or if he could fix fo narrow and confined a boundary to human happinefs.

The face of the country, as far as this place, is for the moft part dull and uninterefting, our road lying chiefly over long and barren mountains, which is pretty much the general appearance of the interior part of North Wales, of which Bala is nearly the center; few living creatures cheer thefe dreary fcenes, but here and there a miferable hut, that ill conceals its wretched inhabitants, and a few poor fheep, thinly fcattered over the fteep fides of the mountain, or picking the fhort grafs from the

almoft

almoſt naked ſummit of the ſhaggy rock, we congratulate ourſelves, therefore, on our preſent ſituation, and on having left behind us the worſt part of our tour; but there are ſome places which muſt be excepted from this general cenſure, and theſe I ſhall briefly take notice of. We ſlept at the King's Arms at Roſs, which was formerly the habitation of that celebrated charaćter who uſually goes by the name of the " Man of Roſs." He was truly a friend to the human kind.—He gave his wordly goods, as far as they would go, to the unfortunate ; and his beſt wiſhes and unqualified compaſſion to all ; his memory is ſtill revered, and his loſs ſtill lamented. I cannot omit ſending you a few lines which my fellow traveller ſcribbled upon a window ſhutter, unlike the general ſtyle of compoſition which ſuch places abound with :

C 2   " Richer

" Richer than mifers o'er their countlefs hoards,
Nobler than kings or king-polluted lords;
Here dwelt the Man of Rofs.   O traveller hear,
Departed merit claims the rev'rend tear;
Friend to the friendlefs, to the fick man health,
With generous joy he viewed his modeft wealth :
He heard the widow's heav'n-breath'd prayer of
     praife,
He mark'd the fhelter'd orphan's tearful gaze ;
And o'er the dowried virgins fnowy cheek,
Bade bridal love fuffufe its blufhes meek.
If 'neath this roof thy wine cheer'd moments pafs,
Fill to the good man's name one grateful glafs,
To higher zeft fhall mem'ry wake thy foul,
And virtue mingle in the ennobled bowl.
But if like me thro' life's diftrefsful fcene,
Lonely and fad thy pilgrimage hath been,
And if thy breaft with heart-fick anguifh fraught,
Thou journeyeft onward tempeft-toft in thought,
Here cheat thy cares—in generous vifions melt,
And dream of goodnefs thou haft never felt."

Montgomery is a neat town, and pleafantly fituated; but except St. Afaph, it is
one of the fmalleft capital towns in the
king's dominions. In the neighbourhood
of Welfh Pool, upon a moft beautiful emi-
nence, ftands Powis caftle, formerly called
Pool

Pool caftle, from its vicinity to Welfh Pool; it was built A. D. 1110, by Cadogan ap Bledhyn, who was not long fuffered to enjoy it, before he was murdered by his nephew Madoc. Such horrid crimes, however, were fo familiar to thofe days, and fo little regarded, that they were frequently committed with impunity, and the offenders might always efcape by a fine or difpenfation. The caftle commands an extenfive view of a fertile vale, through which the Severn, yet in its infancy, rolls gently along. The road from thence to Llanvilling is very intricate, and we contrived to lofe our way more than once, notwithftanding we had been told it was as ftraight as an arrow; we wanted about five miles of the latte place, when we met with an honeft Cambrian of a very refpectable appearance— we did not fail to make fome enquiry of

C 3   him

him concerning our road; he ſtopped his
horſe very politely, and informed us that
he was then returning from Llanvilling,
the place of his nativity, which he had not
ſeen for more than twenty years before;
he added that we ſhould find an excellent
inn, and plenty of the beſt ale in Wales;
he then wiſhed us a pleaſant walk, aſſur-
ing us we ſhould meet with princely accommodations, and earneſtly recommend-
ing the ſign of the *goat*, at the ſame time
adviſing us to make uſe of his name, for
Owen ap Jones ap Evans was as well
known as any name in Wales. I relate
this little anecdote to you, becauſe I think
the character of a people is beſt delineated
by their actions, and their leading features are as completely developed by an
action, or an anecdote of themſelves, apparently inſignificant, as they could poſſi-
bly be in five hundred philoſophical pages

upon

upon the nature of climate, fituation, or government, and the phyfical caufes and effects they may have upon the human genius and difpofition. We were much diverted with the whole of our walk to Llanvilling, particularly with the fmall but pleafant river Verniew, which we croffed. It was late when we arrived, and were much difappointed with refpect to thofe excellent accommodations our honeft friend had hinted at, for we could get nothing but dry bread and bad cheefe, poor cheer for two hungry travellers that had fcarcely eat any thing fince breakfaft.

Llangunnog is fingularly fituated, furrounded on all fides by barren and fandy hills. The place confifts only of a few houfes, amongft which there is a fmall building ycleped a church, where once a week a fermon is delivered in the Welfh language.

language. Whilft we were at dinner in
a little ale-houfe (which by the bye was
the only one in the place), we had a
glance at the clergyman, who happened
to enter the houfe at that very time ; his
appearance altogether befpoke an inferiority of condition, difgraceful to that refpectable body of which he was a member ; upon obferving us, he abruptly went
out, while our landlady informed us, with
an air of triumph, as if he was fomething
fuperior to the reft of mankind, that "that
was the parfon." He was ftanding near
the houfe when we went out, and wifhing
to enter into converfation with him, I de-
fired him to inform me which was the
direct road to Bala ; he appeared fome-
what confufed, and waving his hand towards the way we had enquired for, an-
fwered only by the monofyllable " that,"
and walked haftily away. I felt much
hurt,

hurt, and at the fame time a great degree of admiration, both at his truly laconic anfwer, as well as at his manner of addrefs, in which pride feemed to be ftruggling with poverty; in fuch a fituation any degree of fenfibility would be to him rather a misfortune than a bleffing. Fixed to a fpot in which there could be no one proper for his company, or capable of his converfation, he might be driven to pafs his evenings, for the fake of fociety, with people very far inferior to him, and by degrees lofe thofe finer qualities of the mind, that refinement of action as well as of thought, which properly diftinguifh the gentleman from the honeft but blunt peafant, or the induftrious mechanic. I fhould not have mentioned this circumftance, but that it bears fome credible teftimony to the common report of the fhameful and fcanty provifion made for the Welfh clergy; which by no means enables them

to

to affume that character fo effentially neceffary to the minifters of chriftianity. I do
not wifh to infinuate that there is any dif-
grace in poverty, but certainly the ignorant
and uninftructed too frequently treat their
teachers with a refpect proportioned to
their appearance; and if this be true, it
calls loudly for laws and regulations which
fhall be more favourable to the lower
clergy in general. The act of parliament confines the falaries of curates within twelve and fifty pounds per annum,
whereas it ought to have been proportioned either to the duty performed, or the
value of the benefice itfelf. Let us take
one inftance—a curate ferves two church-
es ten miles diftant from each other;
whilft the incumbent, or vicar, who holds
them both, and receives for the joint value
of the tithes, five hundred pounds per annum, allows his curate, who does all the
duty,

duty, only forty pounds per annum. This cannot be confidered as an adequate com- penfation, even for the labour; and add- ing the refpectability and appearance of the profeffion, it is indeed contemptible and infignificant *.

Bala is fituated upon the borders of a

* The following extract is a fingular confirmation of the above ftatement.

" The curates of the undernamed places, were lately elected by the truftees of Mr. Stock's liberal donation, to receive ten pounds each, viz.

The curate of Llanfwrog, in Anglefea, 5 young children, and 25l. per annum.

Ditto of Beguiley and Bettus, Radnorfhire, 9 young children, 35l. per annum.

Ditto of Michaelftone Vedow, Monmouthfhire, 8 young children, 25l. per annum.

Ditto of Llangadfan, Montgomeryfhire, 6 young children, 25l. per annum.

Ditto of Ireby, in Cumberland, 8 young children, 25l. per annum.

Ditto of Llanvair, Monmouthfhire, 4 young children, 13l. per annum.

Ditto of Burwarton and Wheathill, Shropfhire, 7 young children, 30l. per annum.

Ditto of Abernorlifh, Caermarthenfhire, 8 young children, 18l. per annum.

The

large lake, eleven miles in circumference,
and four and a half long. It abounds
with pike, perch, trout, and other fish;
the country around is grand and fublime,
but not interefting; ftupendous mountains feem " to mix their heads with
dropping clouds," but with refpect to cultivation, or even verdure, they are entirely
deftitute; every neceffary article of life is
here more than commonly reafonable; fifty
pound at Bala would go as far as an hundred in moft parts of England. We were
yefterday much diverted with a curious
political converfation carried on at the inn,
in the room which we in part occupied,
at a table by ourfelves; at another, were

The curate of Sebergham, Cumberland, 8 young children, 30l. per annum.
The curate of Silian, Cardiganfhire, 6 young children, 15l. per annum.

This valuable charity is annually given to ten poor
curates who have large families; and reflects the
higheft honour on the worthy donor."

feated

feated the clergyman, the excifeman, the attorney, the apothecary, and I fuppofe, by his appearance, the barber of the place, &c. thefe were met upon bufinefs over a bowl of punch, which feemed to conftitute the chief part of it; whilft in an oppofite corner of the room, two more decent looking people were enjoying them-felves in a fimilar manner. The clergy-man gave aloud " Church and King," as a toaft, and foon after one of our neighbours at the other table, propofed " General Wafhington" to his friend; this created a great commotion amongft the large party; for the clergyman immediately ftanding up gave as his fecond toaft " may all *Demicrats* be *gullotin'd*," when the other filling *his* glafs, added, " may all fools be gullotin'd, and then I knows who'll be the firft;" after this enfued a violent and dreadful battle of tongues, in

D   which

which thefe people excel in an extraordinary degree. The clergyman defended his toaft, on the grounds that it fhewed his zeal in a good caufe, forgetting that it was neceffary firft to prove the merit of the fentiment, as united by him, and after that, to fhew that his zeal was beft made known as a clergyman, by his benevolent and truly pious wifh. But majors and minors were things which this zealous and humane defender of his church and king had little regard for. The clamour at length became fo loud, that we foon withdrew ourfelves from the fcene of contention, and left the combatants to fettle the point in the beft manner they could; though it feemed to me that it required more fophiftry than the clergyman had difplayed, and more wit than the other poffeffed, to juftify or even excufe themfelves. From hence the traveller may

eafily

easily visit the two Arrans, *viz.* Arran, Mowddwy, and Arran Penllyn, both of them of a stupendous size, but inferior to Snowdon, Cader Idris, or Paenman-mawr. We intend to proceed to-morrow as far as Llangollen; but I will not defer closing a letter which I have imperceptibly lengthened far beyond my original design; and believe me, my dear friend, that I subscribe myself with sincerity,

Your's affectionately, &c.

I. H.

LET-

LETTER II.

DENBIGH, JULY 14, 1794.

IT was late in the evening when we left Balá, and therefore, contrary to our original intentions, we took up our quarters for the night, at the Druid houfe, a folitary place only eight miles diftant from that which we had laft quitted; and early the following morning we purfued our journey to Llangollen. The face of the country now became more interefting. The fcene gradually affumed a lefs rugged appearance; the dark brown mountain, and the defolated heath, foftened by diftance, formed a beautiful contraft to the wild and irregular fcenery that fucceeded. We felt our fpirits, which had before been depreffed from the barren and gloomy

country

country we had traverfed, now much exhilarated, and we feemed to breathe a freer air. There is an analogy in nature throughout, from the moft torpid ftate of vegetable exiftence to the moft refined fubtlety of animal life; and he who has not confidered this attentively, will be furprifed, upon reflection, to perceive that his own felf importance is folely derived from the contemplation of external ob-jects; for deprive him of thefe, fhut him out from nature, fuppofe him to be to-tally unacquainted with the harmony of this beautiful fphere, he muft confider himfelf in the moft contemptible point of view, created for no purpofe, endued with powers of perception and reafoning for no poffible good; his would be a mere comfortlefs ftate of exiftence, with a mind that could have no adequate idea, if any at all, of the deity; his would be a fitua-

tion

tion unworthy the character of his fpecies, and little elevated above the brute creation. Certainly there is a chain of caufes and effects throughout every creative world, whether mineral, vegetable, or animal; and all has an effect upon the mind of man. When we approach a defolate and cloud-capt country, an uncultivated and dreary fcene, what is the caufe that we frequently feel a damp upon our fpirits? Why does it affect the mind, as it were, with a leaden weight, and deprefs the active fprings of the imagination? It is from the analogy which nature, under every form fhe may affume, bears to the varied life of man. Memory backward turns her view, and affimilates the objects before her, to fome certain paffage of our life, that impreffes upon the mind a fhade of melancholy or joy, according as thofe paffages may have

been

been marked with pleafure, or with pain.
It is not therefore that there is any abfo-
lute impreffion made upon the mind, from
the fcene before us, whether it be bright
with funfhine, or overcaft with clouds,
but it is memory which affociates to it
fome event, or tranfaction of former years,
which, though fcarcely perceptible, is the
caufe of fuch an effect. Our road wound
along the banks of the river Dee, which
falls murmuring over its pebbled bed at the
foot of the mountains, whofe fteep fides are
covered with wood of the largeft growth,
here and there the fhaggy rock, more than
half concealed by the furrounding foliage,
peering its broken fummit beyond the
moft extended branches, and threatening,
by its fall, to obftruct the courfe of the
river beneath; whilft the fpreading beach-
tree, and mountain afh, that are found in
great abundance upon its banks, dipping
their

their flender branches in the ftream, and above all, upon the lofty fummit of a conical mountain, the caftle Dinas Brân, rifing in ruined majefty; at once afford an interefting fpectacle of grandeur and fublimity, as well as of beauty and cultivation. Llangollen is moft delightfully fituated, but the place itfelf has nothing to boaft of, except a very good inn which fortunately belies its appearance. We were entertained, upon our arrival, by a celebrated Welfh harper, who tuned his ftrings to fo Orphean a meafure, that a crowd foon collected round the door of our little inn, fome of whom began to dance after the ruftic fafhion of their country; the fimplicity of former times ftruck forcibly upon my mind, and brought back the pleafing recollection of thofe happy ages, when riches and luxury had not corrupted the heart of man; but when

all

all mankind were brothers, and the intereſt of one became the intereſt of all. It
afforded me a ſatisfaſtion I had never before experienced, to find myſelf amongſt
a people, who aſt with all the ſimplicity
of nature ; totally deſtitute of the aſſumed
appearance, and artificial manners of more
modern times. The Welſh muſick aſſi-
milates to the genius of the people, and is
in general wild and irregular, but often
plaintive, and always affeſting ; for the
harp is perhaps more calculated to expreſs
the extremes of paſſion than any other in-
ſtrument ; it is aſtoniſhing with what ſkill
and execution it is ſometimes played upon,
and with what enthuſiaſm the country
people liſten to it ; inſomuch that I have
no doubt the fine tones of a Cramer, or
a Clementi, would be totally diſregarded
by theſe honeſt people, for the humble
ſtrains of a blind Welſh harper. The
muſical

musical amateur of the present day would
despise so vulgar a taste; for with him the
Italian school is alone supportable; I dare
not therefore profess myself an admirer of
simple and unaffected musick, or, in other
words, prefer that which penetrates to the
heart, to that which goes no farther than
the ear; because I should be immediately
condemned as a Goth, Vandal, or bar-
barian. I shall venture however to observe,
that it appears to me there can be no ab-
solute criterion of musick; that being the
best, which touches the passions, and af-
fects the feelings in the greatest degree,
by any assemblage of sounds whatsoever;
and if this be true, a Welsh harp, or an
Irish bagpipe (risum teneatis amici) well
executed, is infinitely superior to all the
fiddle strings and kettle drums of Italy or
Venice.

There are two roads from Llangollen
to

to Wrexham, one on each fide of the
River Dee; the beft is that on the right,
which we took; but it is rather the
longeft. This road is carried upon the
high grounds, from whence the profpect is
delightful. The river, winding through
the valleys, fometimes intercepted by a
rifing ground or thick wood, then opening full upon the view, the luxuriance of
nature is richly difplayed through the
whole landfcape. Upon the hill above us
were feen the dark figures of the miners;
the confufed noife of the men, who were
preparing to defcend thefe gloomy ca-
verns, and of the bufy team, returning
with its ponderous load; while the thick
volumes of black fmoke, that continued
to afcend into a clear and beautiful atmo-
fphere, formed an uncommon and ftriking
contraft. On the other fide, the river,
ftealing through the valley, had, by its
overflowing,

overflowing, contributed to give it the richeſt appearance of fertility; in ſome places the mower, almoſt buried under the high graſs, often pauſed from his labour; in others, the ſharp found of the grinding ſtone, the loud laugh, or toil-ſubduing ſong, were frequently heard: on the ſides of the oppoſite hills were ſcattered the modeſt hamlets that owned theſe induſtrious peaſants; behind us, at ſome diſtance, the whitened ſpire, and part of the little town we had left, were ſtill viſible; whilſt over all, the ſetting ſun caſt its ſoftened tints, a part of the valley only being ſhaded by the inter-poſition of a neighbouring mountain, whoſe ſummit ſtill retained in glowing colours the laſt rays of the departing day. On the right, a little farther on, there is a fine view of Chirk caſtle, and on the left, of Winſtay; the firſt, the ſeat of Mr.

Middleton,

Middleton, the laſt of Sir Watkin Wil-
liam Wynne. About half way from Llangollen to Wrexham, we croſſed a bridge
where the two roads meet, and then we
bad adieu to the River Dee, which kept
its courſe afterwards to the right of us.
Wrexham is a large populous and well
built town; there is a very elegant tower
belonging to the church, reputed to be a
great curioſity. But I have very little
pleaſure in viewing the works of art; and
indeed, human ingenuity of any kind or
deſcription, excites rather my admiration
than my love : as far as they have contributed to ſoften the manners of mankind,
it is well ; but have they not alſo tended to
corrupt and deprave them? If, on the one
hand, they have contributed to their
wants and conveniences; on the other,
they have encouraged the exceſs, and afforded an unbounded gratification to the

E   ſenſual

fenfual paffions; the fine arts, like fo many handmaids, fhould ever be ready to attend, but not to command; to foften manners, but not to render them luxurious.—From Wrexham our road became lefs interefting; and for ten or twelve miles, prefented nothing to recompence the fatigue of a long and tedious walk, until we had afcended a very high hill, when the vale of Clwyd, in all its beauty, unfolded upon the fight: it appeared like a moving picture, upon which nature had been prodigal of its colours. Hamlets, villages, towns, and caftles, rofe like enchantment upon this rich carpet, that feemed covered with wood and enclofures; in the midft of it, at the diftance of about five miles, the town of Ruthin, partially appeared from the bofom of a moft beautiful grove of trees; the vale on each fide being bounded by a chain of lofty mountains, and far off,

on

on a bold and rugged promontory, ftood
Denbigh, with its ftrong fortrefs, the undif-
puted miftrefs of this extended fcene.
The great defeĉt of the vale, is its want of
water; the little river Clwyd, which winds
through it, not being perceptible at any
diftance, and in dry feafons quite choaked
up ; though on the contrary, in wet and
rainy weather, it foon overflows the whole
country, fwelled by the torrents from the
furrounding hills *. The land in the vale
lying low, and confequently fwampy, is,
upon a nearer examination, rather coarfe.
We dined at Ruthin; where there are fome
remains of a caftle, and reached Denbigh
yefterday evening. This town is well built,

---

* This delightful vale is of an oval fhape, twenty-fix
miles in length, and about eight wide in the broadeft
part ; it is wholly bounded with high hills, excepting
towards the Irifh fea, where it ends in a marfh at
Rydland.

Gentleman's Tour through Wales, &c.

and

and the principal ſtreet which is on the ſlope of the hill, is broad and clean, but there are very indifferent accommodations to be met with. After tea we took a walk to view the caſtle, whoſe venerable walls, riſing high above the town, command a magnificent view of the whole vale.

The ſituation of this caſtle is admirably deſcribed by Churchyard, who lived in the time of Queen Elizabeth, and wrote his travels through North Wales in familiar verſe.

" This caſtle ſtands on top of rocke moſt hye,
A mightie cragge, as hard as flint or ſteele;
A maſſie mount, whoſe ſtones ſo deepe doth lye,
That no device may well the bottome feele.
The rocke deſcends beneath the auntient towne,
About the which a ſtately wall goes downe,
With buyldings great, and poſternes to the ſame,
That goes thro' rocke to give it greater fame."

It was built in the reign of Edward the
Firſt,

Firft, and garrifoned, in the time of Charles the Firft, by the royalifts; but was obliged to furrender to the parliament army, after a gallant and vigorous defence; the breaches in the walls are vaft, and ferve to fhew the ftrength and thicknefs of their conftruction. The royal and unfortunate fugitive, Charles the Firft, after his retreat from Chefter, took up his abode for one night in this caftle. But it was deftined that he fhould be the firft facrifice to freedom; and neither armies nor caftles, walls nor cannon, could protect him from the hands of juftice; or prevent an oppreffed people from avenging upon him not only his own, but the fœdal defpotifm, and worfe than papal tyranny, of five preceding reigns. Wretched muft be that government, and the people that live under it, when it becomes neceffary to reftrain the encroachments of arbitrary power, at the point of

the

the fword; or to exact obedience to the
will of the fovereign from the cannon's
mouth. Denbigh is more of a venerable,
than a magnificent ruin, and would, of itfelf, have amply repaid me for all the fatigue I had undergone ; I would not willingly exaggerate the accounts of what I
have feen, or endeavour to paint things
otherwife, than as they really are; for I
am fenfible, that the reader too often ac-
quires falfe ideas of places and things,
from the pompous defcription of the traveller, who thinks himfelf obliged to relate
fomething of the marvellous, in order
that the world may not ridicule him, for
crofling feas or traverfing defarts, in fearch
of what he might have eafily feen at home;
and yet it often happens, that fcenes, though
too highly coloured, may have had that appearance, to the eye of the fpectator, at
the time he defcribes them; and that

what

what appears to him extremely beautiful to-day, may to-morrow ftrike the imagination in a very different manner; for much depends on the hour of obfervation, and the temper of mind we are in, to enjoy the obje&ts before us. I cannot avoid relating a ludicrous circumftance, that took place, whilft I was amufing myfelf with wandering about the caftle; and obferving the effe&t of the fcenery, through the huge breach, or broken arches, that looked over an almoft perpendicular precipice, into the vale below. The moon was juft rifing in the horizon, when I perceived two gentlemen approach; they feemed to be expatiating upon the beauty of the fcene, and in very earneft converfation with each other, one of them frequently repeating parts of Shakefpear, which I could not diftin&tly hear, with a very theatrical tone and a&tion. But I

cannot

cannot exprefs to you how much I was delighted, when, upon their nearer approach, I overheard the theatrical gentlemen propofe to his companion (as he had brought his flute in his pocket), to retire into a remoter part of the caftle, and play fome *foft airs*; God blefs thee for the thought, faid I to myfelf, amidft thefe folitary ruins, by the faint light of the moon, to liften to the foft cadence of diftant mufick, ftealing its mournful melody, on the deluded ear like " founds of heavenly harmony," muft be altogether a foothing and romantic occupation for the mind, accompanied with thofe pleafing fentiments of melancholy, that are better felt than defcribed. Having chofen a convenient fituation, and prepared myfelf for the fupreme pleafure I was about to receive, lo! this romantic difciple of Orpheus, *ftruck up* the tender air of *Corporal Cafey*. I quitted

ted the caftle in an agony of difappoint-
ment, and left thefe romantic gentlemen
to enjoy their *foothing concert*, and folitary
fituation, undifturbed. I returned, however, foon after, and found to my great
fatisfaction that the coaft was clear : nothing could be more awfully grand, than
the fcene before me, which I furveyed
with a degree of admiration, not totally deftitute of a fuperftitious fear. The venerable appearance of the whole fabric ;
walls, and battlements, rifing in ruined
majefty ; broken arches, half covered by
the creeping ivy, and enchanters night-
fhade, high gothic windows, which but
difplayed the horrible gloom that reigned
within ; the mouldering tower, fhook by
every ftorm, affording an afylum to the
owl, the bat, and the raven, lone tenants
of thefe defolate manfions ; whilft the
moon burfting from a dark cloud, threw a

partial

partial gleam upon the pile, and ferved, by its feeble light, to difcover the deep gloom of the remoter parts. At the fame time, a fearful ftillnefs every where prevailed, except that it was now and then interrupted by low folemn founds of wind, that feemed to figh amongft the diftant turrets; the intermediate paufes imprefling upon my mind a mixture of awe and veneration, which the furrounding fcenery greatly contributed to encreafe.

The poft is going out, fo that I have only time to tranfcribe the following lines upon Denbigh caftle, with which I fhall clofe this letter,—Adieu.

UPON THE RUINS OF

DENBIGH CASTLE.

Now fad, and flow, borne far on dufky wing,
Sails the ftill eve; night from her ebon throne
Slow rifing, fcatters wide her myftic fpells
O'er the tir'd world; and from yon murky clouds
Gleams

Gleams the pale moon, diffufing holy light
Through many a midnight ifle and filent fcene.
Much mufing on life's changeful fcene, I view,
Proud pile! thy tempeft beaten towers, that rear
Their heads fublime, and to the angry ftorm
Bid bold defiance, though their aged brows
Bear vifible the marks of ftern decay;
While fuperftition, with a phrenfied eye,
And wildering fear, that horrid forms furveys,
Affright the lonely wanderer from thy walls.

    Far hence thou bufy world, nor here intrude
Thy founds of uproar, arguing much of care
And impotent alarms; behold, fond man,
This feeble monument of mortal pride,
Where time and defolation reign fupreme
With wildeft havock—o'er the folemn fcene
In filence paufe, and mark this pictur'd truth;
That not alone the proudeft works of man
Muft perifh; but as this tow'ring fabric,
That lifts its forehead to the ftorm, till time
And the wild winds fhall fweep it from its bafe;
Pafs but a few fhort hours—the dream of life
Is fled, and to the cold grave finks man's faded form.

LET-

LETTER III.

ABBER, July 16, 1794.

THE laſt letter which I wrote to you,
my dear friend, was dated from Denbigh. I now reſume my pen from a ſpot
far different indeed, but not by any
means deſtitute of beauty. We quitted
the above-mentioned place with great re-
luctance, and often looked back upon its
venerable ruins, contraſting them in different ſituations, with the ſurrounding
objects. Intervening hills had ſcarcely
ſhut them from our view, before we entered upon a wide common, from whence
a delightful proſpect (terminated only by
the ſea), lay extended before the eye;
on the edge of the common ran the rapid
river Elwy, which we croſſed, over a

very

very beautiful bridge, with one noble
arch.—The view of the river with its
rocky fhore, excavated in the moft romantic manner—and the fimple cottage
embofomed within the dark wood that
rofe above it, formed an interefting per-
fpective fection through the arch of this
bridge.

St. Afaph is a fmall neat town, fituated upon the declivity of a hill, at the
foot of which runs the river Clwyd.
About three miles on this fide of Holywell, there is a very extenfive profpect.
From the fummit of a hill, we commanded
a view of the Dee, incorporating its waters with the ocean. Far beyond, though
confiderably involved in a thick fmoke,
appeared Liverpool, the feat of bufy
commerce; and to the right, Park-gate, a
favourite watering place, the abode of

pleafure,

pleafure, and of fong. I could not help
fmiling at the prefent appearance of the
river Dee, compared with what it was
when I formerly beheld it; at that time
unconfcious of its future greatnefs, it mur-
mured over its craggy bed, or fmoothly
glided through the meadows and rich paf-
tures, where numerous herds of cattle
were feeding, or feeking to allay the fultry
heat, in the midft of the ftream. Many
humble cottages rofe upon its banks,
prefenting interefting pictures of content
and happinefs; children bufily employed
in picking floes from the bufhes that
hung over the ftream, or amufing themfelves with throwing pebbles into the
water, thus fporting with time, and
" recklefs that age and forrow with icy
hand hung over them." In another place
a rough alpine bridge, thrown acrofs the
river, afforded a precarious paffage to the

cottager,

cottager, in hafte to reach his fimple home, and fhare with his little family the produce of his daily toil.—Far different did it now ftrike the eye:—a noble river pouring its mighty waters into the bofom of the ocean; towns and cities rifing upon its fhores, big with the vanities of man, and fleets of merchantmen proudly floating in with the tide, laden with the wealth of the world.

Holywell is a clean built town, furrounded by a moft beautiful country. There is a manufacture eftablifhed at this place, that once gave bread to thoufands, but alas! the loom is now forfaken for the fword, and the bufy roof of induftry exchanged for the fickly tent.

The town and neighbourhood, as might be expected, abound with numbers of

F 2

poor

poor women and children, who are half starving, whilft their hufbands, fathers, and brothers, are glorioufly fignalizing themfelves in the fervice of their country; and if by chance the ruthlefs fword of war fhould fpare the poor man's life, and fend him to his long wifhed-for home, with the trifling lofs of a leg, or an arm, he will at leaft have the confolation of re-flecting that he might have loft them both; and fhould his ftarving family, in the bitternefs of want, by chance re-proach him for his incapacity to relieve them, he will no doubt filence their mur-murs, and turn their forrow into joy, by reminding them, that it was in the glori-ous caufe of their king and country that they fuffered. But not to treat with le-vity a fubject fo very ferious, let us take another example; the poor foldier, who at the conclufion of a long war, reduced

by

by famine, ficknefs, and fatigue, and dif-
abled by cruel wounds, is finally compelled to drag on a miferable exiftence in
an hofpital, or a work-houfe; or is returned upon the wide world, without
hope, and void of expeƈtation, a burden
to himfelf, and ufelefs to all around him.
It would be pale and fickly confolation
to his drooping fpirits, to be informed
that his were wounds and fufferings worthy of a foldier and a man, becaufe they
were acquired in his country's caufe. Humanity muft weep over viƈtory when pur-
chafed upon fuch terms, and tremble for
the fatal effeƈts of defolating war, where-
by immediate mifery is occafioned to thoufands, and eventual forrow infliƈted upon
millions.

What hope for man! o'erwhelming war,
   Uncommon furies in his train,
O'er heaps of carnage rolls his car,
   And Europe mourns her thoufands flain:

What

What hope! amidſt difaſtrous days
* When freedom's temple totters to its baſe,
And with earth's vileſt brood diſhonoured ſcience ſtrays†.

The author, in his beautiful ode, has
finely introduced this apoſtrophe, to the
unfortunate ſituation of his country, involved in a calamitous and deſtructive
war abroad; and its happineſs and tranquillity ſubverted and deſtroyed at home
by the real or pretended exiſtence of
plots and conſpiracies, it matters not
which, for they are equally to be lamented; becauſe they have, in either caſe,
been the cauſe of ſuſpending the great
bulwark of Engliſh liberty, the Habeas
Corpus Act; and of giving riſe to many arbitrary meaſures, which nothing but the
moſt abſolute neceſſity could juſtify. He

* Alluding to the ſuſpenſion of the Habeas Corpus
Act, and to the fate of Muir and Palmer.

† Ode on a diſtant proſpect of Cambridge.

has

has alfo expreffed his indignation at that feverity of punifhment, almoft unequalled in hiftory, which was inflicted upon two men, whofe real intentions *deferved ap-plaufe* inftead of difgrace*.

The well of the virgin St. Winifred is well known for its fingular virtue of curing the blind, the lame, and the pal-fied. Innumerable are the trophies of old crutches, wheel-barrows, fpades, &c. that decorate this venerable building ; the grateful teftimonies of thofe various cures

* The author of thefe letters does not mean to throw out any reflection upon the criminal laws of England. It is well known that the law which ban-ifhed Muir and Palmer for fourteen years, compofed part of the Scotch jurifprudence. The author is con-vinced that the *common law* of this land is its greateft glory, that it is a fword to the guilty, and a fhield to the oppreffed ; and that as long as the *Habeas Corpus* Act remains unviolated, and the *trial by jury* pure and independant, no time or tyranny can ever efface the liberties of his country.

which

which its miraculous waters have performed. The ftory is as follows:

" St. Winifred, a beautiful and devout virgin, having fled from a young man called Cradock, the fon of a king named Alane, who would have difhonoured her, he purfued and overtook her near the church, where, on her refufal to yield to his defires, he with his fword cut off her head. On the fpot where it fell, there fuddenly fprang up a fair well, yielding a vaft quantity of exceeding clear water, yet famous for its wondrous virtues in healing diverfe difeafes ; at the bottom of the well are to be feen ftones fpotted with blood, which ftains, cannot be effaced, and round its fides grows mofs of a marvellous fweet odour.

" St. Bueno, a holy man, coming from
the

the church to the fpot where the body lay, and finding the murtherer, who had not power to move from thence, he firft replaced the head, and then by his prayers raifed Winifred to life, and ftruck Cradock fuddenly dead, whofe body turning black, was inftantly conveyed away by fiends; foon after St. Bueno going to Ireland, ordered St. Winifred to fend him an annual token, which was to be put on the ftream of the well, from whence it would be carried to his place of refidence, fifty miles beyond the fea."

Rudland is remarkable for its caftle. The founder, as well as the precife time in which it was founded, is quite uncertain. It is fituated upon the banks of the Clwyd

Abergeley is a fmall watering place, about

about half a mile from the fea.—They have a ftrange cuftom there, that has an air of great indelicacy to a ftranger; which is, that the inferior orders of people commonly bathe, without the ufual precautions of machines or dreffes; nor is it fingular to fee ten or a dozen of both fexes promifcuoufly enjoying themfelves in the lucid element, regardlefs, or rather unconfcious, of any indecency. Not being myfelf accuftomed to this mode, I chofe to retire farther up; but it is very unpleafant bathing, being a flat level beach, and neceffary to wade a quarter of a mile into the fea before one can arrive at any comfortable depth.

The approach to Conway, from the oppofite fide of the water, is extremely grand. The caftle (built by Edward the Firft, A. D. 1284.) ftands upon a rock,

the

the foot of which is wafhed by " Conway's
foaming flood." I there paid a vifit to the
tombs of my anceftors, fome of whom lie
buried in the church belonging to the town.
Obferve that this vifit muft not be at-
tributed to fuperftition, or ought of peculiar veneration for their memory, but the
effect of mere curiofity; for there is a fingular monument of one of them, who was
the father of forty-one children, by two
wives. I took down the infcription with
a pencil, and then left my prolific anceftor
to his uninterrupted repofe.

We ftrengthened our party at Conway
by the addition of two of our particular
acquaintance, whofe plan being fimilar
to our own, we united our interefts, and
fet out from Conway, each provided with
a ftick, knapfack, and trowfers. We certainly prefented to the aftonifhed Cambrians a very formidable appearance;

sometimes

fometimes exciting their rifible mufcles, and fometimes being the occafion of much alarm, particularly amongft the children, who always took us for Frenchmen; but the country people, in general, looked upon us as recruits. Our walk to Abber was fingularly beautiful; this road was formerly almoft impaffable, but with incredible labour and expence, it has of late years been rendered more commodious. The deep and gloomy paffes between the ftupendous mountains, that feemed ready to clofe over our heads, had an appearance truly terrible and grand; and almoft induced me to give credit to what Cambden has afferted,—that two fhepherds might converfe together upon oppofite mountains, and be a day before they could meet. The pafs of Paenman Mawr, that was once attended with fo much danger to the wary traveller, is now perfectly fafe. We arrived late in the even-

ing

ing at Abber, which confifts but of three
or four houfes; the inn is very commodious, but, at the fame time, the accommodations are rather extravagantly pur-
chafed. We rofe early the following
morning for the purpofe of afcending to
the top of Paenman Mawr, and ordered
dinner to be ready for us at two o'clock,
expecting to have returned by that hour;
but we reckoned without our hoft, for the
expedition took up nearly the whole of
the day, and we thought ourfelves happy
to return when we did.—We rafhly took
the refolution to venture up this ftupendous mountain without a guide, and therefore unknowingly fixed upon the moft
difficult part to afcend, and confequently
were continually impeded by a vaft number of unexpected obftructions. At length
we furmounted every danger and difficulty, and fafely arrived at the top; but

G   the

the fatigue we had undergone, and the excessive heat of the day, deprived us, in a great degree, of that pleasure we should otherwise have received from the prospect, and occasioned a tormenting thirst that we were not able to gratify; for water was an article which we searched for in vain. Preparing, in the utmost despondency, to descend, we accidentally turned over a large flat stone that concealed a little spring, which, thus obstructed, became absorbed under the surface of the earth. The parched-up soldier of Alexander's army could not have felt greater joy in the discovery of his little treasure, than we did of ours. In the course of our descent we incautiously separated; and as it was dusk, I began to be under some apprehension that we might lose ourselves in the intricacies of the mountain; in order to discover their direction, or distance from

me,

me, I frequently repeated their names, and was much entertained with a beautiful echo, which returned the found of my voice in three different directions; had I been inclined to fuperftition, many circumftances would have contributed to raife its full effect upon my mind, which as it was, bufily employed itfelf in creating images of fear. An awful filence fucceeded the laft vibrations of the echo, which was only interrupted by the diftant barking of the watch dog, that proceeded from the lonely hut of the fhepherd; or the fhrill fhrieks and hootings of the owl and rock eagle.—In the midft of my melancholy cogitations, I fully expected that the genius of the mountain would have appeared to me in fome formidable fhape, and have reproached me with rafhly prefuming to difturb the facred filence of his folitary reign; or at leaft that fome ban-

G 2

ditti,

ditti, more terrible in afpect than ever
Salvator Rofa could have painted, or even
imagined, would have rushed upon me
from behind a rock, and made me pay,
perhaps with life, for my unintentional
temerity. We had the good fortune,
however, to arrive at the inn together,
nearly at the fame time, that is to fay, about
nine o'clock. You may eafily imagine
that the difficulties we had previoufly
encountered, heightened the enjoyments
of our prefent fituation, and we paffed a
very pleafant evening in difcourfing upon
the adventures of the day. There is a
cataract about a mile from Abber, worth
feeing, on account of its precipitous fall;
but it is totally deftitute of wood or
fcenery. This evening we mean to crofs
the ferry into the Ifle of Anglefea, but I
will referve the account of this part of our
journey until another opportunity, or
till

till the experience of new adventures may render a repetition acceptable.—In the mean time believe me, my dear friend, under every circumſtance of time or place, I ſhall ſtill continue my beſt wiſhes for your happineſs, and remain

Your's ſincerely, &c.

I. H.

LET-

LETTER IV.

CAERNARVON, July 19, 1794.

SINCE my laſt, my dear friend, I have encountered ſome difficulties both by land and water, and am, in conſequence, come to a final determination in my own mind, that terra firma is infinitely preferable to that changeable element where Neptune holds his powerful ſway. I muſt acknowledge the dangers of the latter are not by any means ſo agreeable, nor can I view them with that tranquillity which, upon moſt occaſions, I have treated the former; not indeed that I am bleſſed with any great ſhare of philoſophy, although I am always toiling to acquire a little of that neceſſary ingredient to human happineſs;

but

but alas ! the irritation which fuch exercife has upon my nerves, is fo hoftile to
the objeƐt in view, that it drives philofophy to a very refpeƐtful diftance. In the
uncertain voyage of life, fome fail upon
troubled, others on fmooth and gentle
waters, and fome again on ftagnant; and
it is our duty to expeƐt to encounter all
forts of weather : man is at the beft but
a weak being, like a reed to be fhaken by
every wind, and buffeted about by every
ftorm ; fome are better failors than others,
and look upon the angry tempeft with
different degrees of fortitude ; for my part
I muft honeftly confefs that I am at the
beft but a bad navigator, and am often
run afhore with only a cap full of wind.

The following anecdote which I have
accidentally met with, is fo fingular, that
I cannot refrain from fending it to you :

A merchant who lived in the golden days
of

of Queen Elizabeth, had seven or eight
sons arrived at the age of manhood, and
being himself upon his death bed, addressed
them as follows: "Sons," said he (after some
previous discourse), " your voyage through
life may be compared to an outward bound
fleet in time of war, that has a safe convoy to a certain latitude, where they
usually separate, and take different courses;
some navigate one sea, some another, and
naturally meeting with various fortunes,
one encounters storms and tempests ; another runs upon shoals and quicksands ;
and a third, even in sight of port, strikes
upon a rock, and is lost ; whilst few, very
few, smoothly sailing upon the tranquil
tide, gain their destined haven in peace. So,
my sons, I, your convoy, have conducted
you even thus far with honor and safety
to yourselves : I must now leave you for
ever, in all probability to be scattered
wide by many fates ; let each, whatever

course

courfe he may fteer, have virtue for his
pilot, and I truft that his faithlefs fortunes—;" but here the ftory breaks off,
and fo muft I, in order to make an apology,
which, according to the polite rules of
writing fhould now follow, for this unneceffary digreffion.—And methinks I hear
you fay, I am travelling 'tis true; but it is
into the regions of fancy, beyond the
reach of common apprehenfions; I allow
the juftice of the charge, and ftand felf
convicted; but I find it a very hard tafk
to keep within due bounds: for, to purfue
the allegory—in the courfe of a voyage, if
the mafter of the veffel happens to difcover a beautiful ifland, abounding with
all forts of fruit, is he a criminal, or even
an injudicious pilot, if he is tempted to
deviate from his direct track, in order to
gather fome? Or if he hears a Syren's
voice, is he to blame in liftening to it?
when

when to refift, the expedient of Ulyffes
would be infufficient—he muft alfo fhut
out the imagination.

The village of Abber Conway, ufually
called Abber, from whence I dated my
laft letter, is fituated upon the ftraits of
the Menai, that at high tide is there about
four miles acrofs; but when the water is
out, it appears perfectly dry; for the fea
retires fo far back, that it only leaves
a channel of a quarter of a mile, or
thereabouts, in breadth : all the reft is a
complete flat, and confequently the tide
overflows it very rapidly. There are
ftated times to pafs this ferry, which one
fhould be very exact in obferving, for ten
minutes may be of the utmoft confequence.
The clergyman of the place accompanied
us to the boundaries of this wildernefs of
fand; he gave us the neceffary directions
for

for our paffage, which were only to keep
a white houfe in view that belonged to
the ferryman on the Anglefea fhore, and
to make what hafte we could, fince there
was no time to lofe, for we had four
miles to walk over this frightful defart
without fhoes or ftockings, having been
advifed to pull them off; for being regu-
larly overflowed every twelve hours, great
part of the road is neceffarily wet and
dirty. We had fcarcely got half way, before it began to grow thick and foggy.
The little village of Abber, which we had
juft quitted, was no longer perceptible;
and nothing behind us was to be feen,
but the fteep and fhaggy mountains of
Paenman Mawr, and thofe known by the
general name of Snowdonia, with the
dark vapours floating upon their fides;
and very foon even thefe became no longer
diftinguifhable, but as one huge mafs of
clouds.

clouds. Myself, and another of the party, had considerably outwalked the other two, who had loft fight of their land-mark, and were fteering their courfe much too far to the right; when we difcovered their miftake they were not fo vifible to us, that we could tell what they were; all that we could difcern, was fomething very dark, moving in a different direction to us; confequently we haled them, and waited till they came up to us, and we agreed to part company no more.—Darknefs had now overtaken us in good earneft, and we could fee nothing, nor hear any thing, except the noife which the fea made in its approach, that alarmed us not a little; at length, to our infinite fatisfaction, we diftinguifhed the voices of the ferrymen, who were luckily waiting on this fide of the paffage. When they heard us, they were extremely impatient

for

for our arrival, and continually called to us to make hafte, which we wanted no monitor to urge us to do ; we therefore made towards the fpot from whence the founds came, which we conjectured to be about the diftance of two hundred yards from us, but were unluckily intercepted by a fmall channel, already filling very faft with the fea. We did not hefitate long, for in fact we had no alternative, and therefore boldly ventured through ; it was fortunately only about two feet deep, and rather more than ten yards broad. We congratulated each other upon finding ourfelves fafe in the boat, though dripping wet, and fhivering with cold. Like the Ifraelites, we had paffed through the fea on dry land ; but we had run a great rifk of experiencing a fimilar treatment with Pharaoh and his hoft, from that unmannerly element. When we arrived at

H   the

the inn at Beaumaris, we made a fire
that would have roafted an ox, and ordered a fupper fufficient for ten aldermen.
Upon opening the window on the following morning, I obferved the fea had covered all thofe immenfe flats we had fo
lately, I will not fay with dry feet, walked
over.

The firft Edward, ambitious of emula-
ting the actions of Alexander the Great,
entertained the daring project of building
a bridge acrofs thefe ftraits, and thus
unite Anglefea with Wales. That proud
monarch, like the infolent Xerxes, vainly
conceived he could control the raging
elements ; and the trouble, expence, and
impracticability of completing fo vaft a
work, was clearly, but in vain, reprefented
to him : chance, however, effected what
reafon had been unable to do ; for at the

very

very time that he was giving orders for the undertaking, fome frefh difturbances broke out elfewhere, and diverted his attention from fo wild and vifionary a fcheme.

Beaumaris is a dirty fea-faring town; here is another of king Edward's caftles built, A. D. 1295; it is in tolerable pre fervation, but the eye is difgufted with new repairs; a fine old tower is fre- quently patched with modern mafonry, in which the workman has barbaroufly fhown his art, in the nice difpofition of yellow bricks and mortar : add to this, the inhabitants have made a bowling-green within its walls.—The guardian genii of venerable ruins, muft furely have been afleep when thefe impieties were com- mitted.

From

From Beaumaris we croffed the ifland, with which I felt myfelf greatly difappointed; I looked around me in vain for thofe awe infpiring fhades and venerable temples where the Druids ufed to perform their myfterious rites, that filled the wondering multitude with fear, and infufed, even into their enemies, a degree of refpect and veneration.

The account given by Tacitus of the expedition of Suetonius, againft this ifland, is the moft ftriking picture of the character of the Druids, and probably more to be relied upon than any other; for veracity conftituted no fmall part of the merit of that excellent hiftorian.

* "Igitur monam infulam incolis va-

* Tacit Annal Lib. 14.

lidam,

lidam, et receptaculum perfugarum ag-
gredi parat. - - - - - - - - -
Stabat pro litore diverſa acies, denſa ar-
mis viriſque, intercurſantibus feminis: in
modum furiarum, veſte ferali, crinibus
diſjeꞔtis, faces praeferebant. Druidœque
circum, preces diras ſublatis ad cœlum
manibus fundentes, novitate aſpeꞔtus per-
culere milites, ut-quaſi haerentibus mem-
bris, immobile corpus vulneribus praebe-
rent. Dein cohortationibus ducis, et ſe
ipſi ſtimulantes, ne muliebre et fanaticum
agmen paveſcerent, inferunt ſigna, ſter-
nuntque obvios, et igni ſuo involvunt."

"He thereupon prepares to attack
Mona, an iſland powerful on account of
its numerous inhabitants, and affording a
place of refuge to thoſe who fled from the
enemy. - - - - - - - - - - -
- - - a motley army ſtood oppoſed

to

to him upon the fhore, thronged with warriors and prepared with warlike inftruments, the women running up and down, and bearing torches before them, after the manner of the furies, in the drefs worn at their funeral folemnities, and with difhevelled hair ; the Druids every where pouring forth the moft dreadful imprecations, with hands uplifted to heaven, terrified the foldiers with the novelty of fuch a fpectacle, who, as if fixed to the fpot where they ftood, yielded their bodies immoveable to the wounds of their enemy. At length, at the exhortations of the general, and alfo encouraging each other, that they fhould not be intimidated at that female and frantic multitude, they advance their ftandards, overthrow all who oppofe them, and plunge the Britons into their own fires."

By

By the bye this laft was an act of the moft unjuft and unneceffary cruelty in the Romans, who feem only to have been inftigated to it by the demons of revenge; for when we confider that the deluded multitude who oppofed their invafion, were in reality fighting in defence of every thing that was valuable in their domeftic, and of every thing that was dear and venerable in their public life; that they beheld the temples of their gods impioufly polluted, and their facred groves violated and profaned; can we feel furprifed, or rather was it nor natural that they fhould refift the fury of an enemy, preparing to trample upon their rights, their liberties, and their religion? And if in general, we regard the conduct of the Romans with refpect to the conquered nations, we fhall find that the moft cruel and rapacious fpirit characterifed all their

military

military tranfactions. They led the un-
happy victims of their perfecution in barbarous triumph to the capital, and felt a
more than brutal pleafure in liftening to
the groans of the untaught and defence-
lefs children of nature, the naked inhabitants of the wilds and forefts of the moft
uncivilized and unpromifing regions.
Their inhumanity and cruelty is only to be
equalled, in more modern times, by the
conqueft of Peru and Mexico, and the
taking of the ifland of St. Domingo by
the Spaniards, which has fixed an indeli-
ble blot of infamy upon that nation ; and
by that difgraceful and abominable traffic
that fubfifts to this day in the Weft, of
bartering our fellow creatures at a public auction, and fubjecting them to the
difgraceful dominion of the moft unfeeling
of tyrants.

Very

Very few traces of the temples and habitations of the Druids are now to be found; fome old ftones, fhapelefs and without order, here and there, indicate that there might have ftood on thefe fpots the rude and fimple piles, where the primæval inhabitants of this ifland folemnifed their religious ceremonies; and this is all that now remains of that once celebrated order of priefthood, which overfpread the northern regions of Europe. Strange fatality! that a fyftem of religion fo founded on prejudice, and rivetted in fuperftition and ignorance, and fo intimately blended with the political governments of thofe times, that it appeared capable of triumphing over that invifible mutation to which all human eftablifhments are liable, and of oppofing Chriftianity itfelf, fhould now be fo loft, fo forgotten, that little more than a few fhape-

lefs

lefs ftones, and the uncertain teftimony of
oral tradition, remain to fatisfy us of the
influence that extraordinary religion once
poffeffed over the human mind:

"Illi rebus divinis interfunt, facrificia
publica ac privata procurant, religiones
interpretantur - - - - - - -
- - - - fere de omnibus controver-
siis publicis privatifque conftituunt, fi quod
eft admiffum facinus, fi cædes facta, fi de
hereditate, fi de finibus controverfia eft
iidem decernunt, præmia pænafque conftituunt *."

"They prefide over all facred ceremonies; they adminifter both public and
private facrifices; they are the interpre-
ters of all religious affairs. - - - - -
- - - - - - - They for the moft

* Cæfar in Gall, Lib. 6.

part

part decide in all public and domeſtic controverſies; if any crimes are committed, if any ſlaughter is made, whether they are diſputes concerning hereditary right, or the boundaries of their poſſeſſions, the Druids always decide upon them; they alſo determine rewards and puniſhments."

This is a general account given by Julius Cæſar of the Druids of Gaul. He ſlightly mentions thoſe of Britain; only taking occaſion to obſerve, that the manners and ceremonies of theſe people are almoſt every where the ſame. Their powers of divination were alſo in great reputation, but the mode of making their obſervations was truly horrid and barbarous. Their ceremonies, according to Tacitus, were performed " in groves, ſacred to the moſt cruel ſuperſtitions; for they offered up their ſacrifices upon altars

ſtained

stained with the blood of their captives;
and it was usual for them to augur according as the blood of the human victim followed the sacred knife that had inflicted
the wound."

Anglesea (though it is called the granary
of Wales) appeared to us as one continued picture of desolation; and for
twenty miles of our road through it, we
could not discover more than five or six
corn fields, and the grass land so misera-
bly poor, that it starved rather than fed
its hungry inhabitants. We undoubtedly
did not see the country to the best advantage, because the excessive heat of the
summer had parched up the ground, and
occasioned a general appearance of dearth.

" Amlwch is a small sea port, from
whence the copper (that is found in the
Paris and Mona mines, which are not

more

more than a mile from the town), is
fhipped to London, Liverpool, &c. The
Mona mine produces the fineft ore; they
alfo make quantities of copper from old
iron (for a particular account of the
whole procefs, fee the Scotch Encyclo-
pedia, Pennant's Hiftory of Wales, &c.)

Thefe mines have an appearance un-
commonly grand and ftriking—a vaft
yawning chafm, difplaying full to the
view of the aftonifhed ftranger its ful-
phurous contents; hundreds of workmen
employed in a variety of different occupations; fome boring fhafts, others felect-
ing the ore, which is flung up to the top,
or, if I may ufe fuch an expreffion,
ufhered into the world in little bafkets.
In fome places the chifel and the pick-
axe find room for employment; in others
the men are feduloufly engaged in blow-

I   ing

ing up large pieces of the rock by means
of gunpowder, the report of which rever-
berating from fide to fide, in this immenfe
cavity, occafions, fuch a tremendous ex-
plofion, that all nature feems to tremble
to its center.—Upon the whole thefe
mines bear an apt refemblance to the
infernal regions, and, like the peftilence
from the pit of Acheron, the fulphur
which iffues from them, fpreads defolation
around, fo that not the flighteft veftiges
of verdure are to be traced in the neighbouring fields.

We dined yefterday at Gwyndn, on
the great road to Holyhead, which is
called by the natives Caer Guby, on account of St. Kybi, a holy man, who lived
there A. D. 308; but none of us expreff-
ing any inclination to fee that place, we
left it on the right, and fteered our courfe

nearly

nearly South, through the center of the ifland. Gwyndn fignifies, from its name, a place of hofpitality at the expence of the lord; and, in truth, it anfwers, in fome refpects, to its title even now; nor muft I forget to pay my tribute of thanks to the hoftefs, a fine old lady, who payed us the utmoft attention, and appeared particularly folicitous about us; fhe gave us her bleffing at our departure, with a thoufand admonitions not to lofe ourfelves. We left this hofpitable inn with regret, and arrived " poft multa pericula," at Hoel Don Ferry, a fingle houfe, where we were obliged to fleep, or, fpeaking more accurately, to lie down, for to fleep was totally impoffible. It was a miferable hut; but we contrived to procure two beds, though the good woman was for putting us all into one. We croffed the ferry yefterday morning, after a fleeplefs night,

I 2

happy

happy to quit this inaufpicious ifland, where fortune had not been over prodigal to us of her favours. The road from this ferry to Caernarvon, winds along the fhores of the Menai, and the fcenery would have amply repayed me for the fatigue and mortification I had undergone, had I then been in a humour to have enjoyed it; but true it is, that when we cannot enjoy ourfelves, we are not much difpofed to be fatisfied with any thing around us; the fineft objects lofe their beauty; and what at other times would have afforded the higheft gratification, are in thofe hours deprived of their relifh. We reached Caernarvon, or Caer-ar-fon (fignifying a walled town), to breakfaft; and it was not until I had eaten, or rather devoured, a certain quantity of toaft and butter, that I began to recover the accuftomed tone of my fpirits. I intended to have clofed this

letter

letter with an account of our tranfactions as far as the time of our departure from this place ; but muft defer the remainder till my next, for fome particular bufinefs has fallen upon my hands, which obliges me for the prefent to fubfcribe myfelf,

Your's, &c.

I. H.

LET-

LETTER V.

OF all the ruins which Wales has yet
prefented to me, the caftle of Caernarvon is the moft noble and magnificent.
" Vaft as the pride of its founder," it
evinces the warlike and invincible genius
of the firft Edward, of whofe military
prowefs this country, as well as Scotland, furnifh fuch numerous and melancholy proofs. Thank heaven, thefe fa-
bricks of defpotifm are at length either
levelled with the ground, or prefent a
memorable leffon to mankind of the fu-
tility of human ambition.

This caftle was erected in order to fe-
cure the paffage into the Ifle of Anglefea,
and to curb the people of the mountains,
where

where the brave and hardy Britons had
taken refuge from their infulting conquerors, refolved to prefer freedom and
independance to eafe and fervitude. The
eldeft fon of Edward was born here, and
he was prefented to the Welfh as their
future prince. Such enormous buildings,
abftractedly confidered, excite only my
abhorrence; becaufe they have occafioned
the exercife of a great deal of tyranny,
and ufelefs expence, and have been of no
poffible advantage to any nation; but
have, on the contrary, afforded fo many
afylums wherein the fword of tyranny
might take fhelter; and were chiefly calculated to keep the furrounding diftricts
in awe and fubjection. Every caftle that
now remains is a monument of fhame to
our anceftors, and of the ignoble bond-
age under which they bent: and hence
in part arifes that fatisfaction, which the
mind

mind is confcious of feeling, in contemplating their ruins; for an affociation naturally takes place; and the recollection of the feudal vaffalage and flavery of former days, is accompanied by the pleafing circumftances of the relative profperity and freedom which we now enjoy. From this place we made a party of three, and croffed once more into Anglefea, where my ill ftars feemed to have pre-ordained that I fhould meet with nothing but misfortunes. One of my companions was a very fkilful botanift, and his botanical furor induced him at all times to defpife danger and difficulty, when in purfuit of a favourite plant, and this was the object of our prefent enterprize; but we had fcarcely fet foot on that inhofpitable fhore, before it began to rain with great violence, and very foon growing dark, we were obliged to make the beft of our

way

way back again. This ferry is two miles
acrofs, and the water was much agitated,
fo that without the addition of the rain,
which came down in torrents, the fpray
of the fea would have completely made
us wet through; but, in the midft of our
diftrefs, we were agreeably interefted by
a fight as beautiful to us as it was
novel; the furface of the water fuddenly
affumed a luminous appearance, now
and then relapfing into an impenetrable
gloom, and then again re-lumined, it
conveyed to the mind fome idea of what
the poets defcribe of Phlegethon in the
fhades below. By the time we had
reached our inn I had loft my voice, and
gained a fore-throat; the following morning it was no better; but under fome
hope that exercife would cure the complaint, was induced to continue our tour
to Bethkelert, which we reached that afternoon;

ternoon; the whole walk being more fingularly romantick than any I had yet
feen, and compelled us to make many a
paufe, in order to enjoy and contemplate
its beauties. About half way, we paffed
over Llyngwennyn bridge, and immediately found ourfelves in a fertile valley,
terminated by a wild and irregular caf-
cade, one branch of which contributed
to turn a mill that was almoft concealed
within the wood, which formed a kind
of amphitheatre to this picturefque and
interefting fcene; a little further on a fine
lake opened full upon the view; and not
far from this another fmaller one. The
road winds along the banks of both.
Bethkelert is a fmall village, or rather
hamlet, fituated at the foot of fome prodigious high mountains, which feem to
encircle it on all fides, whilft the ftream
or torrent, that had accompanied us all

the

the way from the firſt lake, here begins
to be of more conſequence, and forcing
its way between theſe ſtupendous hills,
with a continued and conſiderable de-
ſcent, empties itſelf into an arm of the
ſea, called Traweth-Mawr. As this is
the uſual place from which travellers
make the aſcent of Snowdon, we determined to do the ſame, and in purſuance
of this reſolution ſet off at eleven in the
evening, though it was quite dark, and a
very rainy and ſtormy night; however, there
was a probability that it would be fine in
the morning; and that hope was ſuffi-
cient to make us undergo a few inconveniences; but in attempting to find the
guide's houſe, which was five miles from
our inn, and ſituated quite out of the
road, at the foot of the mountain, we
became completely bewildered: in this
perplexity we were directed by the glim-

mering

mering of a light to an habitation, which, with extreme difficulty and dange , we contrived to reach. It was a fmall hut, and its inhabitants, if we might judge from the impenetrable filence that reigned within it, were all afleep. It was fome time before we could prevail upon them to open the door, and anfwer to our entreaties for a proper direction; at length an elderly man appeared, to whom we endeavoured to make known our grievances; but alas! he only fpoke his native language, and did not underftand a word that we faid: However, by frequently repeating the guide's name, " Ellis Griffith," and pointing to Snowdon, at the fame time giving him a glimpfe of a fhilling, we with much difficulty made him comprehend us; and putting himfelf at our head, he became our conductor. In about half an hour we found ourfelves

at

at the door of another fmall cottage: our
guide vociferated Welfh for fome minutes,
till we were admitted by a good-looking
lad about 17 years of age, who was the per-
fon we had been fearching for: he re-
monftrated againft our afcending that
night, with many weighty reafons, to
which we eafily affented; but to think of
returning to our inn would be madnefs:
we therefore called a council of war, and
it was agreed, that we fhould at all
events ftay where we were, until morning; when, if it fhould be tolerably fair,
we would afcend. Thus determined, we
difpofed of ourfelves in the following
manner; I barricadoed myfelf in a chair,
fo that I could not fall out; two more
repofed themfelves on the benches on
each fide of the fire, and the fourth took
up his " lodgings on the cold ground,"
with an earthen platter turned up-fide

K   down

down for his pillow. As for my part I
was not difpofed to fleep, but took up
the rufh-light, which had been placed for
fecurity on the ground; and to pafs away
the leaden hours of time, pored over an
old Welfh dictionary (which was the only
thing like a book that I could find), till I
was fcarcely able to fee. I could not
help contemplating our fingular fituation
and appearance in this ftrange place: on
one fide, around the dying embers of a
peat fire, my good friends were enjoying
as comfortable a repofe as they had ever
experienced in the moft coftly bed: at
the other extremity of the room, fepa-
rated only by a rug, the venerable own-
ers of this humble cottage lay locked in
each others embraces: whilft I, like Bru-
tus in his tent at Philippi, fat reading by
the mid-night lamp, till the light danced
before my eyes, and the pale fpectre of
the

the night appeared to my imagination. Without doors nought but the " pelting of the pitylefs ftorm" was heard, and the loud roar of the mountain torrents: I recollected fome lines of a favorite author, which I thought applicable to my prefent fituation:

" And when rude bluft'ring winds and driving rain,
Prevent my willing feat;
Be mine the hut that from the mountains fide
Views wild and fwelling floods."   COLLINOS.

Yet while I was contemplating the fcene, under fuch peculiar circumftances, with a mixture of awe and furprife, thefe fimple cottagers lay perfectly indifferent, and unconfcious of any novelty in their fituation. The noife of the cataract was by them fcarcely ever remarked, or ferved to ftrengthen their repofe; mountain floods, abrupt and broken preci-

pices,

pices, were alike viewed by them with the utmoft indifference; fo foon does the human mind become familiar, and accommodate itfelf to any circumftances. Habit and cuftom are even fo powerful as to change the very complexion of things, and render that finally pleafing, which at firft could not be viewed without fear or diflike. The Savoyard will climb from rock to rock, and fearlefs walk upon the brink of tremendous precipices, which we, unaccuftomed to fuch fcenes, cannot contemplate, even at a diftance, without emotion; but, in a little time, we become familiar to them, and ridicule thofe fears we had formerly entertained, for what we can now view with fo much unconcern.

At four in the morning I thought it prudent to awaken the whole party, which

which I effected with some difficulty; we then sallied from our habitation, and made our observations upon the weather, which gave us no encouragement to proceed; however, they determined to venture upon their aërial excursion, more from the hope of finding the plants, for which this mountain is remarkable, than of seeing any thing when at the top: at their persuasions, added to my own inclination, I declined the enterprise, as my cold had considerably increased during the night, and went back again to the inn, where I impatiently expected their return, which did not happen till four in the afternoon. It turned out, as might have been foreseen, a fruitless and fatiguing expedition; for when arrived at the top, they could see nothing but the impenetrable clouds, that almost constantly envelope these huge mountains.

K 3 We

We quitted Bethkelart the following
morning, and purfued the courfe of the
fame ftream I have above fpoken of; that
for nearly two miles rolls with great ra-
pidity at the foot of prodigious high mountains, which rife on each fide of it, almoft
perpendicular from its banks, leaving but
barely room for a narrow road, which muft
have been cut at a vaft expence. The
gentle and murmuring founds of the
water, occafioned by its declivity, and the
obftructions it has to overcome, form
a rude but grateful harmony. Pont Aber
Glaflyn terminates this fublime fcene.
The bridge, and furrounding objects, are
here highly deferving of attention. From
hence we fteered our courfe to the left,
and traverfed the wildeft and moft defolate country that North Wales can boaft
of; for the moft part confifting of vaft
hills, rifing one above another, covered
with

with fhaggy rocks, without the flighteft veftiges of verdure. We reached this place yefterday evening: I am delighted with the fituation, which is the moft retired and pleafing I have ever feen; it ftands upon the borders of a valley fufficiently high to command a view of its whole extent; the Druryd, a fmall, but interefting ftream, winding its folitary courfe, undifturbed, through the midft of it; and, at the lower extremity, a fimple, but elegant bridge, terminates the view. The woods are very picturefque, and cover the oppofite hills to a great extent; gratifying the eye with a conftant variety. Why, my dear friend, has nature placed her moft alluring haunts, her moft delightful fcenes, fo far from the reach of man? Why has fhe prodigally fquandered away upon fo many diftant and uncivilized regions, and upon this favoured country in particular, all her ma-

jefty

jefty and fimplicity? Why has fhe given to a people, who behold, without enjoyment, fcenes of beauty, where, for my part, I could be almoft content to pafs through this ftrange fcene called life, in peace and folitude? I know you will blame me for thus giving way to vifions, which ought not to be realized, and your anfwer I already anticipate (viz.) that man was not made for folitude, or felfifh enjoyments. That our brother travellers, through this tedious journey, call for our affiftance, and have a claim upon our exertions; and that nature would no longer pleafe, no longer afford delight and gratification in her works, if they were every where equally beautiful; or, in other words, were there not barren mountains, fmoky cities, ungenial foils, and unwholefome climates; then would lakes, woods, rivers, fertile valleys, cultivated plains, villages, and

hamlets,

hamlets, be no longer objects of curiosity or admiration.

The inn at Tan y Bwlch is remarkably neat and commodious; we yesterday made an excursion from hence, to view the fall of the Cynfael, one of the most celebrated cataracts in Wales. With much difficulty and danger I climbed up to its tremendous and almost unattainable summit; from whence the water, collected into a body, falls tumbling from rock to rock, and steep to steep, till it reaches a vast pool, or bason, frightfully deep, and so remarkably clear, that the pebbles at the bottom of it may be distinctly perceived, though I could form no judgment of its depth. The scenery at the foot of the cataract, was beyond imagination beautiful; but I will not attempt to give you a particular description of it, because I

have

have neither time nor power to do it juſtice. We leave this place to-morrow morning, and you may conclude, after what I have ſaid, it will be with ſorrow and regret. I ſhall now cloſe this long, and I fear, tedious letter, and be aſſured, I feel myſelf as much as ever,

Your ſincere Friend,

I. H.

LET-

LETTER VI.

ABERISTWITH, July 29, 1794.

THIS is the laſt letter, my dear friend, that I ſhall have the pleaſure of writing to you whilſt I am in Wales; an unex-pected event obliges me to be at Bath in a few days, ſo that I am under a neceſſity of leaving this country ſooner than I had intended; but I will take care and write to you as ſoon as I arrive, with the re-mainder of my tour, together with a few obſervations upon the character of the people.

It was with much difficulty we found our way to Harlech. We made ſome en-quiries at a ſmall village, but in vain; for though we addreſſed ourſelves to many,

we

we could by no means make them underftand. us; all we received in return
was a ftare, immediately followed by a grin,
and concluded with a " tin farcenick,"
which fignifies " no Saxon." We were
obliged therefore to rely upon chance for
our guide, which did not however upon
this occafion befriend us; for, inftead of
keeping to the right upon the hills, we
purfued the left path, that brought us
into an extenfive vale, or marfh, where, at
the diftance of about five miles, we firft
perceived the objects we were in purfuit
of (viz.) the town and caftle of Harlech.
After fome confiderable exertions, we
were obliged to abandon this valley, becaufe it was fo fwampy, and fo much in-
terfected by ditches and drains, that it
would have been, if not impracticable, at
leaft extremely uncomfortable and difficult
to proceed. With great fatigue and perfe-
verance,

verance, we climbed up the almoſt perpendicular, and craggy ſides of the mountain, which bounded that part of the vale,
where we were reduced to the above perplexity, and at length reached Harlech;
for the firſt time heartily fatigued.

The country people have no idea that
a ſtranger can be ignorant of their roads;
we have not unfrequently aſked the way,
and received for anſwer, " that it was as
ſtraight as we could go;" when, in a very
few paces, we have been perplexed by
two roads, one declining to the right, and
the other to the left.—Nor have they
much idea of diſtance; each meaſuring it
by the rule of his own judgment and opinion. It is no unuſual thing to be told,
that the diſtance to ſuch a place, may be
about five miles, " and a pretty good
ſtep;" which pretty good ſtep, generally
proves to be about five miles more.

L

Harlech

Harlech caſtle is nobly ſituated, and, like Denbigh, ſtands upon a lofty promontary, terminating a chain of hills, and commanding on one ſide a view of the ſea, and on the other, a very extenſive vale and proſpect. From its ſingular ſituation, it muſt have been formerly eſteemed almoſt impregnable; and yet we read in our hiſtory, that it was beſieged, and taken, in the time of Edward the Fourth, by the Earl of Pembroke, without the aſſiſtance of gunpowder. We alſo here achieved an exploit, which, beyond all doubt, gives us ſome title to military prowefs; for as there did not happen to be any body in the way, who might open the gates of the caſtle, and our time not permitting us to wait for the ordinary forms of capitulation, we boldly marched up to the aſſault, and ſcaling the walls at four different places, took poſſeſſion of the garriſon, as it were

ſcaglin

by a coup-de-main. But for this daring
outrage, we had well nigh got into an
aukward fcrape; fome of the inhabitants
obferving our operations, and probably
taking us for free-booters, gave the alarm;
and muftering a formidable body of forces,
marched in military array, to difpoffefs us
of our ftrong hold. But we foon pacified
our opponents, and having convinced them
that our intentions were neither predatory
nor hoftile, they retired to an ale-houfe
to banifh forrow, and indulge themfelves,
at our expence, in copious libations of
ale.

There is nothing interefting in the road
to Barmouth, nor has that place itfelf any
ftriking peculiarities, except that the
houfes are fo whimfically built, upon the
fide of a fteep hill, that the inhabitants

fide

may have the advantage, if they choofe, of looking down their neighbour's chimnies. The town ftands upon the fea fhore, and in the feafon is full of company, who refort thither for the purpofe of bathing.

From Barmouth to Dolegelly we were highly gratified; the road wound along a ridge of rocks, that hang over the A-vonvawr, an arm of the fea; which, at full tide, has the appearance of a large lake, furrounded with beautiful woods: The mountains on both fides, but particularly on the oppofite fhore, were ftrikingly grand; and above all, Cader Idris reared its head into the clouds, which, together with the fombre afpect of the evening, and the hollow murmurings of the fea gave an awful fublimity to the fcene that cannot be defcribed.

Dolegelly.

Dolegelly is a large and dirty town: we took up our quarters at the Golden Lion, a good hofpitable inn; and next morning, after breakfaft, procured a guide to conduct us to the top of Caer Idris. We armed him with ftores, and warlike preparations of all kinds (to wit): ham, fowl, bread, and cheefe, and brandy, and began the afcent at nine in the morning, and continued to toil for three hours and a half before we reached the top. But, alas! expectation had again flattered us; for, though it was a moft lovely day in the valleys, yet here we could not fee fifty yards before us; the fummit of the mountain is not of greater extent than the bafe of a common fized room; and, on one fide, falls almoft perpendicularly many hundred yards in depth. When I ftood upon the edge of this precipice, and looked into the frightful abyfs of clouds, it put me in

mind

mind of the chaos, or void fpace of darknefs, fo finely defcribed in Milton, when
the fallen archangel ftood at the gates of
hell, pondering the fcene before him, and
viewing, with horror, the profound ex-
panfe of filence and eternal night:

— — — — — — — — — — — — a dark
Illimitable ocean, without bound,
Without dimenfion, where length, breadth, and heighth,
And time, and place are loft.

The height of this mountain is little
inferior to that of Snowden.—The view
from it, on a clear day, is grand and magnificent. Ireland, the Ifle of Man, North,
and South Wales, lie extended before the
eye like a level map. The whole mountain is apparently compofed of a huge
mafs of ftones, thrown together as a
heap of rubbifh without order or defign;
for, wherever you turn up the fod or turf,
which

which is not in general more than two
inches thick, you come to thefe ftones,
and they are nearly about the fame dimenfions, and have the appearance of
being broken with a hammer. Near the
fummit of the mountain there is no turf,
and what is remarkable, thefe ftones are
fmaller there than in any other place.
Had there been any larger maffy rocks at
the top, it would have afforded a probable
conjecture, that fhivered in the courfe of
time, by lightenings and tempefts, they
might have fallen by piece-meal upon the
lower fides of the mountain. But, as I
have already ftated, there is no appearance of that kind at the fummit, and fuch
a fuppofition muft therefore be excluded.
Nor could an earthquake have caufed the
phenomenon, becaufe we have no teftimony whatever, either ancient or modern,
of any part of Great Britain, having been
fubject

subject to such extraordinary convulsions of nature; and the idea of the flood being the cause, is futile and ridiculous to the last degree; for the vast body of water, which, we are informed, was collected upon the surface of the earth, would, instead of scooping out valleys, and heaping up mountains, have been more likely to have levelled mountains, and filled up valleys. Besides it is not quite clear, that the whole surface of the globe was affected by that sweeping deluge; and therefore Great Britain, from its remote situation, might, as well as any other country, have been exempted from a share of its favours. But it is not my intention to throw down the gauntlet of controversy, with respect to this, or any other subject of scripture history so extremely remote; it is happy perhaps for the authenticity of many parts of that history,

tory, that it is beyond the reach of human teſtimony now to diſprove it.

It is well for me, my dear friend, that I do not live under the paternal government of the inquiſition, either in Venice, or Spain, or Italy, or Portugal, or any other place, where the parental and tender affection of the holy fathers, might ſolely for the preſervation of my ſoul, mercifully condemn my body to the purification of fire. But to return to the mountain, or rather to take leave of it, for I have already kept you too long upon ſo ungenial a ſoil, I will conclude this digreſſion, with the idea of a celebrated philoſopher, who conceived it probable, that, when God had compleated his great work, this beautiful world, out of ſo many rough materials, not knowing what to do with the rubbiſh that remained, he threw it together in various

rious heaps of different magnitudes, juft
as it happened, and thus formed what we
call mountains.

We arrived at the inn, at Towen Merionith, late in the evening; where we
had the pleafure of being fpectators of a
Welfh affembly; they invited us to join
them, but our fatigue was too great
to permit us; added to which our drefs
was not altogether fuitable to the occafion; though, from what I could obferve of
thefe honeft Cambrians, we fhould not
have been very outre in our appearance,
if we had ventured amongft them, habited
as we were. I cannot help relating a remarkable inftance of fimplicity, that happened to me here the fame evening. As
foon as I had got into bed, I found
the fheets were extremely damp, and having fuffered fo much lately in catching
cold,

cold, I thought it a neceſſary precau-
tion, and indeed but common prudence,
to throw them aſide. When the maid
came to take away the candle, ſhe would
not be convinced that the ſheets were
damp: " Lard ſir (ſaid ſhe), it be impoſ-
ſible, for they have been a ſlept in four or
five times within this laſt week." We
left Towen (which is about a mile from
the ſea), yeſterday morning, for there is nothing particularly attracting in that place,
or captivating to the eye of a ſtranger.
It was our intention to have reached
Aberiſtwith laſt evening, but were obliged
to take ſhelter from the fury of a ſtorm,
in a ſolitary houſe, not far from the ferry
at Aberdovy, where we were detained
much againſt our inclinations the whole
night; but we have happily arrived here
this morning without any further obſtacles.
Aberiſtwith is a very reſpectable bathing
place.

place. There are some fine remains of a
castle, that formerly commanded the approach from the sea on one side; and that
to the town, from the land on the other.

The trade of Aberistwith is not by any
means contemptible; great quantities of
coal, and lead, are found in the neighbourhood, and shipped from this port to
different parts of England.

Adieu, my dear sir, and believe me, I
feel the greatest pleasure in subscribing
myself,

Your sincere friend, &c.

I. H.

LET-

LETTER VII.

IN my laſt, my dear friend, I ſaid that you would not hear from me until I reached Bath; but I find I ſhall be detained here till the morning, the weather proving too rough for the paſſage boat, to venture with their cargo of live and dead ſtock, and therefore I cannot better fill up the intervening time than by writing to you.

I did not part from my old companions until we reached Llanindovrey, ſo that we had the pleaſure of ſeeing Pont-ar-finach together, otherwiſe called the Devil's bridge. It is the largeſt cataract in Wales, and well worth the traveller's at-

M   tention.

tention. About one hundred yards from the bridge, there is a houfe of accommodation for company, though I cannot fay much in favour of it; however, it is pleafantly fituated, and overlooks the deep and woody glen, into which, from a prodigious height, the waters of the cataract fall, with a deafening noife. With infinite labour and fatigue, I got down to the bottom of this glen, or chafm. I did not undertake the perilous expedition alone; but neither my companion or myfelf were gratified or recompenfed for our trouble, becaufe the cataract is fo obfcured by bufhes and underwood, that, at the foot of it, it is not all difcernible.

Tregarron is a miferable hole, in the which however we were conftrained to fleep, and to break the windows in our

bed

bed rooms to let in the frefh air. We took a guide from thence to Llanindovrey, over the lonely and tracklefs mountains of Cardiganfhire; it rained hard the whole way, and we had not even the gloomy confolation of feeing a partner of our misfortunes: for, to fpeak within compafs, we neither beheld a fingle habitation, nor even a human creature, for more than twenty miles. From Llanindovrey I journeyed on alone, for the reft of the party not being preffed for time, could make their obfervations at pleafure, having no neceffity for hurrying over the country as I was obliged to do.

Brecknock is fituated on a fmall rifing, above the river Ufk. I cannot do juftice to the beauty of the country, the whole way from Brecknock, to Crickhowel and Abergavenny: it is one continued landfcape, abounding with every rich va-

riety

riety of fcenery, and beautifully inter-
fperfed with hamlets and villas. At
Crickhowel there are fome remains of a
caftle, but at Abergavenny (commonly
pronounced Aberganey), fcarcely any: it
derives its name from the river Gavenni
which there meets the Ufk. To me, who
had but juft quitted the uncultivated and
tremendous fcenery of North Wales, its
rocks, its mountains, and its cataracts;
the fertile hills and cultivated vales of
Brecknockfhire were doubly ftriking;
and the rich features of the latter, heightened beyond the reality from fo lively a
contraft.

Ragland caftle is a very fine ruin,
belonging to the duke of Beaufort; the
road from thence to Tintern, would gratify the moft romantic imagination; the
laft three miles, or more, being a continual defcent through a deep and gloomy
w od,

wood, till the aftonifhed traveller burfts
from the furrounding fcenery full upon
the Wye, that rolls its muddy waves in
rich meanderings through this folitary
glen. The lively picture that immediately offers itfelf to the view, of boats in
full fail, of others landing their cargo,
with the bufy and cheerful cries of the
failors and workmen, was like the effect
of enchantment, and almoft created in
me an imagination, that I had arrived in
another world, and had difcovered a new
order of beings. At fome diftance ftands
the abbey, whofe holy ifles, and melancholy fhades, were once devoted to religious fervour and monaftic difcipline : it
was founded A D, 1131. The monks
were of the rigid order of Ciftertians*.

* At what time chriftianity was introduced into
Britain, it is not correctly known ; but it is certain
that it was in fome degree eftablifhed here, though

continually

We owe to Henry VIII the suppreffion and overthrow of thefe feminaries of bigotry and fuperftition: as long as they

continually perfecuted by the Saxon Pagans, long before the arrival of Auguftin the Monk, who was fent upon a holy miffion into this ifland, A. D. 596. However, the abufes of chriftianity were coeval with its introduction; and this holy father himfelf fet his heart not only on fpiritual but temporal things; for he was created the firft archbifhop of Canterbury: he is alfo accufed of having excited the Saxons to fall upon the Britons, and to maffacre twelve hundred monks of Bangor. Monachifm is fuppofed to have been introduced into Britain by Pelagius, at the beginning of the fifth century.

The contracted limits of a note are infufficient to enumerate the infinite variety of monkifh fraternities, and the crimes they were guilty of: but according to Gregory, their enormities are fcarcely credible. In confequence of the fuppreffion of thefe monafteries in the time of Henry the Eighth, ten thoufand religious were turned into the wide world; and Henry became poffeffed of all monaftic revenues whatfoever; thefe on the whole amounted to fix hundred and forty five monafteries, ninety colleges, and two thoufand three hundred and twenty four chantries and free chapels.

exifted,

exifted, the exertions of genius were fet-
tered and confined; and Europe was
overfpread with one general gloom of religious fanaticifm and intolerance. About
the twelfth and thirteenth centuries,
fome enlightened minds awoke from the
general flumber; but it was a feeble ef-
fort, and the darknefs returned more
thick and heavy than before. Monkifh
pride and cloiftered pedantry every where
ufurped dominion over man.—Learning
and fcience were finally depreffed, and
ignorance became the beft fhield of protection; but truth at length unfolded the
deep veil of hypocrify and prieftcraft—
reafon refumed her empire—the whole
fabric of papal defpotifm fell at once to
the earth; and luft, cruelty, and revenge,
that had fo long been concealed within its
walls, fled at the firft glimmerings of
light; whilft the pure and genuine principles

ciples of Chriftianity rofe as a pillar of
glory upon the ruins, and pointed to uni-
verfal happinefs and peace.

The elegance and lightnefs of the
ftruƈture exceeds any thing of the gothic
architeƈture I ever faw. It occafioned in
me much regret that I was compelled to
pafs over, and to vifit, in fo curfory a manner, a fcene, which, for beauty and fingu-
larity, might challenge nature throughout. I wifhed to have examined more
minutely the venerable remains of this
once celebrated abbey; but the very fabric which I was fo much admiring, in-
dicated too forcibly that I had to deal
with that inexorable and infatiable foe,
called " Time." I felt the conviƈtion, and
with reluƈtant fteps haftened to Persfield,
celebrated for thofe extenfive and magnificent gardens, which have coft fo much
labour

labour and expence heretofore, though now fuffered to run into decay.

Chepftow is a very neat and well fitu-ated town; it has a caftle that might once have been formidable, but is now a complete ruin. Having thus brought my tour to a conclufion, I have the fatisfac-tion to add, that the event has not difap-pointed, or fallen fhort of expectation; and what few difficulties we encounter-ed greatly contributed to heighten our other enjoyments. 'Tis true we have fometimes been obliged to cook our own victuals, fometimes to be content with very fcanty fare, and fometimes with none at all; nor were we ever indulged with down beds, chince curtains, or Turkey carpets; but good health and wholefome fatigue rendered fuch articles of luxury totally ufelefs and unneceffary.

To

To fum up the advantages and difadvantages; I do not hefitate a moment to fay, that were I to make the fame tour again, or one through a fimilar country, I fhould certainly perform it on foot, both from motives of convenience and independency.

Upon the whole I have been as much charmed with the manners of the people, as with the country which they inhabit; there is a boldnefs and originality in all their actions, which marked the conduct, and characterifed the features of their anceftors. A love of liberty and independence is implanted by nature in their breafts, and is cherifhed into maturity upon their mountains and fea coafts by a hardy and defultory manner of life. With refpect to hofpitality, they ftill preferve their original character; the manner of it

is

is undoubtedly much altered, it is lefs
magnificent but more pleafing; the
ftranger is not conducted into a noble
hall, and placed at the right hand of the
chief; no bards attend with the fongs of
times that are paft; the walls are no
longer hung with the maffy fpears of departed heroes, or decorated with the fpoils
of a vanquifhed enemy; the conch does
not found to war, nor is the boffy fhield
ftruck as the fignal to meet the threatening foe. Strange ferocious manners were
blended with the hofpitality of thofe days;
but, happily for mankind, fuch barbarous
features of uncivilized ages are at length
every where humanized into more refined and focial enjoyments. Whether
fociety has not arrived at an excefs of refinement; whether a great degree of refinement is not the parent of vice and
corruption; and if fo, whether an age of
barbarity

barbarity with honefty and virtue, or an age of refinement, with effeminacy, vice, and corruption, is moft defirable, or moft calculated to produce the immediate and eternal happinefs of mankind? I leave to be determined by thofe who have leifure and inclination, to confider with attention fo abftracted a fubject.

The occupation of war, and the amufe-ments of the chafe, have given way to the more domeftic employments of pafturage, agriculture, and fifhing.—Of the produce of their daily labour, the ftranger is gene-rally welcome, and though their poverty is obvious, they refufe every recompence but thanks and civility; I fpeak chiefly of the lower orders of the people; of the higher, or more opulent, the manners are almoft every where the fame.

I cannot

I cannot do better than quote, upon
this occafion, a couple of ftanzas from
Churchyard, who has been a conftant
companion in my walks, and has better
expreffed in poetry the character of the
people in this particular, than I could
have done, had I attempted it, in profe:

Like brethren now doe Welfhmen ftill agree,
In as much love as any men alive ;
The friendfhip there and concord that I fee,
I do compare to bees in honey hive ;
Which keep in fwarme and hold together ftill,
Yet gladly fhowe to ftraunger great good will ;
A corteous kynd of love in every place,
A man may find in fimple peoples face.

Paffe where you pleafe on plaine or mountain
wilde,
And bear yourfelfe in fweete and civil fort,
And you fhall fure be haulft with man or childe,
Who will falute with gentle comely port
The paffers by : on braves they ftand not fo,
Without good fpeech to let a trav'ler go :
They think it dett and duetie franke and free,
In towne or fielde to yeeld you cap and knee.

N   In

In Wales, pride and poverty go hand in hand, and the difpofition of the people is ftrongly blended with fuperftition. When we were at the top of Cader Idris (the etimology of which fignifies the chair of the giant Idris), the guide fhewed us the giant's bed, at which we could not help laughing; the honeft fellow, however, rebuked us for fuch levity, and expreffed his belief as to the identity and exiftence of the giant, at the fame time juftifying himfelf from the authority of a clergyman, who had lately made a pilgrimage to the fame fpot; and, immediately falling down on his knees, began to fay his prayers in a devout manner, and an audible voice; without doubt to appeafe the manes of this tremendous giant, and breathe out a pious requiem to his foul.

The general character of the people is certainly

certainly amiable—their attachments are ftrong and fincere; their paffions and refentments violent, but tranfitory, which is always the charaᵭeriftic of an unpolifhed people. The ingenuoufnefs of nature is fhewn in its real colours, and difplayed in all their aᵭions. They do not trouble themfelves with the politics of the times, or addiᵭ themfelves to the habits of thinking, and the cares of the world they have little concern with; for they are free from thofe occupations, thofe tremulous folicitudes, which engrofs the attention of a commercial people. With refpeᵭ to their language, I am not fufficiently acquainted to give any opinion; to my ear, I muft confefs, it is not very harmonious; but refembles rather the ravifhing founds of a cat-call, or the mufical clack of a flock of geefe when highly irritated. The dialeᵭs are extremely various, and the

difference

difference is often obfervable, even between adjacent counties; but in North
and South Wales, there is fo great a varia-
tion, that they may almoft be faid to be
different languages. Yet, notwithftanding, I feel much pleafure whenever I
hear it fpoken, being the old Celtic
dialect, which, together with the fimplicity of the country people, brings back to
my mind the memory of former times;
but my ideas of them are fo imperfect,
and our knowledge in general, of the
relative virtue and happinefs of our Celtic
anceftors, fo confufed, that I fcarcely
know whether to rejoice that thofe times
are paft, or wifh that they may again return; with refpect to them, and the Welfh,
as they are at this day, there appears to
me to be this material diftinction: the
former knew not what wealth (in the
modern acceptation of the word) was; and
confequently

confequently were ftrangers to many vices attendant upon it. The latter, from their intercourfe with the rich and mercantile parts of Great Britain, have unfortunately acquired a relifh for riches without the means of procuring them: hence arifes that pride which prompts them to conceal their poverty, and that jealoufy of their national charaćter and fituation, which breaks out almoft upon every occafion. The children are remarkably beautiful, and ufually well made, but this only continues during their infancy; for, from the age of ten and upwards, they begin to bear the marks of hard labour, and ftill more precarious fubfiftence.—— A haggard countenance, a reduced appearance, and, in fhort, all the traces of a premature old age * : fad proofs thefe of

---

* Poverty, though it does not prevent the generation, is extremely unfavourable to the rearing of chil-

dren;

poverty and wretchednefs; and but too
true indications of mifery and want, and

dren; the tender plant is produced, but in fo cold a
foil, and fo fevere a climate, foon withers and dies.
It is not uncommon in the Highlands of Scotland, for
a mother who has borne twenty children not to have
two alive. Very few of them arrive at the age of
thirteen or fourteen; in fome places one half of the
children born, die before they are four years of age;
in many places before they are feven; and almoft
every where before they are nine or ten. This great
mortality, however, will be found chiefly amongft the
children of the common people, who cannot afford to
tend them with the fame care as thofe of better
ftation.

Adam Smith's Wealth of Nations."

This excellent writer, whofe calculations are in
general fo accurate and exact, has here ftated facts
the moft melancholy, truths altogether difgraceful to
fociety; hard lot of poverty indeed! and blafted is
the foil, if its influence extends to the untimely and
unmerited deftruction of the human race. The ftale
and hacknied argument, that thefe things are per-
mitted by Providence for fome wife purpofes un-
known to man, muft in this inftance be rejected, becaufe it is apparently a levity of cruelty, to give a numerous offspring to the parent, only to mock and in-
fult

of an inferiority of condition, juſtifiable upon
no grounds whatever, either of revealed
religion, or natural equity. The population of North Wales, compared with its
extent, is very trifling, and unequal. This
may be accounted for from a long chain of
cauſes, but chiefly from the continual ſtate
of diſcord and warfare, in which the chiefs
and princes were always involved, until
the final ſubjugation of Wales by Edward

ſult her with a proſpect of happineſs, and then leave
her to anguiſh and deſpair.

Great Britain is enabled to provide for more than
its preſent population, even without the aſſiſtance of
any external commerce. And Europe, it is well
known, might maintain one hundred millions of ſouls
more than ſhe at preſent does. Government then is
the only remaining cauſe of all theſe evils: government, which ought to remove every obſtacle to population, endeavours to depreſs and retard it ; nor is there
any hope of amendment, while amongſt numerous
other cauſes, the abuſe of eſtates, the rapacity of fi-
nance, and the immenſe eſtabliſhment of ſtanding armies continue to exiſt,

the

the Firſt, and even then, the inhabitants
were treated merely as a conquered people, and admitted to few privileges of the
conquerors ; for it was not till the time of
Henry the Eighth, that they were ſuffered
to have the ſame advantages with Engliſh
ſubjects. Secondly, from the ſituation of
the country, which is too remote for the
Engliſh land trader, and oppoſed to a very
dangerous ſea ; added to which its ports
are by no means ſo commodious and ſafe
as thoſe of England. Thirdly, and prin-
cipally, the barrenneſs of the ſoil, together with the mountainous nature of the
country, and conſequently the great difficulty of land carriage, which is the chief
obſtacle to its internal trade. Theſe are
certainly ſerious impediments to the
flouriſhing ſtate and proſperity of the
people ; but they are not beyond a re-
medy, and it ought to become the duty

of

of the legiflature to provide every poffible
means of improvement, and to endeavour,
by wifdom and attention, to remove or
diminifh thofe local inconveniences which
are a bar to the happinefs of the fociety
of any particular diftrict or tract of land
over which that legiflature has dominion;
eftablifh manufactures, hold out rewards
for agriculture; in fhort, increafe the population of the country by the moft approved
methods; wealth will follow of courfe,
commerce will be extended, and the now
defolated mountains of North Wales may,
at leaft, repay the labour of cultivation,
though they can never be fo productive
and flourifhing as thofe of their fouthern
neighbours. We know that Attica was
little better than a defart of fand; yet, encouraged by wife laws, the inhabitants
overcame the obftructions of nature, and
it quickly flourifhed as the garden of
Greece.

Greece. We know the almoft infur-
mountable obftacles that the great Czar
Peter had to encounter; yet, in fpite of
thefe, affluence fmiled upon the induftrious
exertions of his fubjects, directed by his
wifdom to ufeful employments: the arts
found an afylum in the frozen regions of
Ruffia, and, from a land of poverty and
defolation, it became a great and flourifhing empire; but the fole end of governments feems to be forgotten, and, inftead
of having for their great and ultimate object, the happinefs and advantage of that
fociety by whom they were inftituted;
they now feem calculated only for the
advantage of a few; and the legiflators
of nations are become the individual
brokers of public property; which, with
the lives of mankind, are fquandered
away, as ambition or caprice may rule
the hour, and dictate to their councils.

You

You will perceive, my dear friend, that I have not entered into minute and particular descriptions—I have neither given you a detail of sieges, nor prefented you with a genealogy half a mile long—I have not defcribed a feaft, nor filled up my pages with infcriptions from old tomb ftones; but if you wifh to derive information on thefe heads, I refer you to the pompous defcriptions of Young, and to the diffufe and voluminous work of Pennant. The world is doubtlefs indebted to the latter for his excellent hiftory of Wales, but it is ftill a hiftory, and has too much of the detail in it to afford me any gratification in the perufal.

I have ftudioufly avoided dwelling upon any thing which bore an analogy, or refemblance to works of art, or unproductive ambition. To fearch out nature in all

her

her various forms, has conftituted my
chief delight ; and to find her in her wildeft
attitudes, has proved to me the higheft
fource of gratification and enjoyment.

I hope, and fully expe&t to fee you very
foon at Cambridge. My beft wifhes attend you, and believe me to be, with the
utmoft fincerity,

Your affe&tionate Friend,

I. H.

APPEN-

APPENDIX.

I T may not be unacceptable to fome of my readers, to lay before them a few general obfervations with refpect to this country.

NORTH WALES

IS DIVIDED INTO SIX COUNTIES.

	Contents in fquare miles.	Towns.	Parifhes.
Caernarvonfhire -	430	5	68
Denbighfhire - -	670	4	57
Flintfhire - - -	250	2	28
Merionethfhire - -	790	4	37
Montgomeryfhire	860	6	47
Anglefea - - -	180	2	74
	3180	23	311

O   The

The market towns in Caernarvonſhire, are Carnarvon, Aberconway, Krekith, Pulhely, and Nevin. It has beſides one city, Bangor.

In Denbighſhire, are Denbigh, Ruthin, Wrexham, and Llanroſt.

In Flintſhire, Holywell, and Caerwis, with one city, St. Aſaph. Flint has no market, but ſends one member to Parliament.

In Merionethſhire, are Harleigh, Dolgelle, Dinaſmouthy, and Bala.

Montgomeryſhire contains Montgomery, Llanvilling, Welſhpool, Newtown, Machynleth, and Llanydlos.

Angleſea

Anglefea has Beaumaris, and New-burgh.

No. of fquare miles in Wales   7011
Ditto in North Wales - - 3180
Ditto in South Wales - - 3831

The population of North and South Wales, are together eftimated at about three hundred thoufand fouls, fo that it will appear there are not upon the average, quite forty-three inhabitants to each fquare mile. I regret much that I have not been able to learn the exact propor-tion of population between North and South Wales; there is, however, no doubt that the latter has by much the largeft fhare. The Ifle of Anglefea contains fifteen thoufand inhabitants, and has ra-ther better than eighty three to each fquare mile; but it is the moft populous

O 2   part

part of the north divifion of our princi-
pality. The total amount of the wafte
lands in Wales, is computed to be about
1,629,307 acres, and great part of this is
ftated to be incurable ; but I am inclined
to believe that if two or three regiments
of foldiers (inftead of fpending in bar-
racks a life totally unproductive to themfelves, and ufelefs to fociety in every inftance, except for the heroic and benevolent purpofes of murder, rapine, and oppreffion), were fet to work upon them at
a fhilling each per diem, exclufive of their
pay, the country would, in a fhort time,
affume a very different afpect. The price
of labour is greater in South, than it is in
North Wales, and yet in Caermarthenfhire, which is a fouthern county, la-
bourers are only paid ten pence a day in
fummer, and find their own diet, and
eight pence in the winter months. The
land

land tax a few years ago produced
43,752l.

There are numerous mines of coal,
flate, copper, &c. that are a great fource
of employment to the poor.—What trade
they have, is, for the moft part, inland, and
confifts chiefly in horned cattle, lead, copper, and coal. Great part of the land,
and particularly in Cardiganfhire, is wild
pafture, and, in its prefent ftate, only fit to
feed that hardy kind of cattle fo peculiar
to the country itfelf; confequently fheep,
cows, &c. are very cheap, and will continue fo until agriculture flourifhes more
than it does at prefent; or, in other words,
until it becomes more profitable to extend
tillage, and fow feed for the food of man,
than dedicate the rude and natural produce of the earth to the nourifhment of
cattle; for, in proportion to the extenfion

O 3

of

of agriculture, the price of cattle will be advanced, becaufe the number is thereby diminifhed, and the demand for them greater. The Welfh are probably defcended from the Belgic Galls, and hence called Galles, or Walles, *i. e.* Strangers. The country was alfo formerly inhabited by three tribes of Britons, the Silures, Dimetæ, and Ordovices. It preferved its independency until the thirteenth century.

There are two circuits, viz.

North Eaft } containing { Flint, Denbigh, Montgomery,
North Weft   Anglefea & Caernarvon.

Wales fends twenty-four reprefentatives to parliament, twelve for the counties, and the fame number for the boroughs.

If the traveller wifhes to fee Bangor, he muft crofs the Menai from Anglefea

at

at the Bangor ferry; but we had been informed that there was fcarcely any thing worthy of particular notice at that place, which account has been fince confirmed to me, by a gentleman with whom I am well acquainted, and who, in company with fome others, made a fimilar excurfion to our's, and in a fimilar manner. It is from his notes that I am enabled to give fome account of Llanberis. The road from Bangor to Llanberis is over fome ftupendous mountains, commanding, as one might have expected, a very extenfive, and not an uninterefting profpect. The vale of Llanberis may contend the point of fuperiority, with refpect to beauty, perhaps with any in Wales; the mountains on one fide being entirely without verdure, and rifing almoft perpendicular from the vale, whilft thofe on the other fide appear to be highly cultivated;

the

the vale itfelf confifting moftly of fine pafture ground, fome fmall lakes at one
extremity, and a few ruftic cots at the
other; here is alfo a copper mine in the
hands of the Macclesfield company. From
Llanberis to Caernarvon, which is about
ten miles, the road lies at firft over high
and unpleafant mountains, and is afterwards fucceeded by a low flat, equally
dull and difagreeable.

Eight miles from Dolegelley are the
falls of the Caen and Morthway. The
higheft part of Snowdon is called the
Wyddfa, from whence, according to Pennant, its moft credible altitude above the
level of the fea, is one thoufand one
hundred and eighty nine yards. The
height of the Cader above the green at
Dolegelley is about nine hundred and
fifty yards. The road to Machynleth, by
the

the pool of Three Grains, is for the moſt part piƈturefque and beautiful. The town, for a Welſh one, is rather neat ; from hence to Aberiſtwith, is a pleaſing and rich country, through which flows the river Dovey.

There is a remarkable cuſtom which the Welſh ſtill continue, that I cannot forbear mentioning : When a marriage is about to take place amongſt the middling and lower orders of people, it is uſual to invite all their friends and relations of every defcription, who, when they take leave, prefent the bridegroom with fome fmall prefent, of one or two ſhillings, which, however, they have a right to de-mand again after a certain fpace of time ; the intent of it being probably to enable the new married couple to buy ſtock, or engage in fome buſineſs that may allow

them

them foon to repay the fmall donations of their friends. It is called "a bidding," and is drawn up in the following form.

"My only fon John has lately entered the facred ftate of union, and a bidding is fixed on the occafion, on Tuefday the 7th day of October next, in the village of Conwyl, when and where your good company and benevolence are highly folicited, which will be cheerfully acknowledged on a fimilar occafion, and efteemed a peculiar favor conferred on,

Your moft devoted

humble Servants,

JOHN JONES, Senior.
JOHN JONES, Junior.

CONWYL,
Sept. 13, 1794.

P. S. Mr. and Mrs. Lewis, of Pantyrhaidd, Mr. Jones, of Clynadda, Mr. Evan Harries,

Harries, of Nant-yr-olchfa, and his brother, David Harries, of Llandre, unite us in complimenting all with their fincereft gratulation.—The young man's parents requeft that all their donations of the above nature may be retaliated then."

In the courfe of our tour I had often occafion to regret that I knew nothing of drawing; the pencil may find room for continual employment in the romantic views of North Wales; but without profeffing myfelf either a poet, a painter, or a botanift, I felt highly gratified at the magnificent fcenery which that country every where difplays. Equally delighted with the elegant fimplicity of nature, but not fo familiar with its productions as another, I cannot find the fame fources of intellectual acquifitions. Undoubtedly the antiquarian and the botanift have a

wide

wider field of inveſtigation, and a more en-
larged page of ſcience is conſtantly difplayed to their view. The poet and the
philoſopher are more abſtracted in their
obſervations, find other principles for the
materials of thought, and apply the rude
unconnected objects of their contemplation, as ſo many foundations, upon which
to build the light fabric of fancy, either in
the regions of moral, political, or meta-
phyſical ſpeculation; but where theſe
are united, nature muſt amply repay her
obſerver, and be at once an inexhauſtible
mine of information and amuſement.

A
L I S T
OF
T O W N S, &c.
WITH
THEIR DISTANCES FROM EACH OTHER.

CAMBRIDGE	0
Oxford, three weeks	90
Glocefter *	47
Rofs *	16
Hereford	12
Leominfter *	16
Bifhop's Caftle *	25
Montgomery	7
Welfh Pool	9
Llanvilling *	12
Llangunnog	18
Bala *	12

254

The

Brought over   411

Caernarvon * . . . . $4\frac{1}{2}$

Bethkelert ** 12

Pont Aberglaflyn 1

Tan y Bwlch * 7

Rhaidr Du 3

Tan y Bwlch ** 3

Harlech 9

Barmouth * 10

Dolegelly * 10

Cader Idris 7

Towen Merionith * 12

Aberdovy 5

Ferry * . . . . $1\frac{1}{2}$

Aberiftwith * 9

Pont ar Finach 12

Tregarron * 15

Llanindovrey * 21

Trecaftle 9

———

562

Brecknock

	Brought over	562
Brecknock		10
Crickhowel		13
Abergavenny *		6
Ragland		8
Tintern Abbey		8
Persfield		4
Chepſtow		2
Old Paſſage *		3
Ferry		1
Briſtol		12
		629

THE END.

www.ingramcontent.com/pod-product-compliance
Lightning Source LLC
Chambersburg PA
CBHW020544270326
41927CB00006B/719